How to Dismantle the English State Education System in 10 Easy Steps

How to Dismantle the English State Education System in 10 Easy Steps

Terry Edwards
& Carl Parsons

Winchester, UK
Washington, USA

JOHN HUNT PUBLISHING

First published by Zero Books, 2020
Zero Books is an imprint of John Hunt Publishing Ltd., No. 3 East St., Alresford,
Hampshire SO24 9EE, UK
office@jhpbooks.com
www.johnhuntpublishing.com
www.zero-books.net

For distributor details and how to order please visit the 'Ordering' section on our website.

Text copyright: Terry Edwards and Carl Parsons 2019
Cover: Linocut image by Gillian Fairbanks, 2019

ISBN: 978 1 78904 430 0
978 1 78904 431 7 (ebook)
Library of Congress Control Number: 2019948302

Design: Stuart Davies

UK: Printed and bound by CPI Group (UK) Ltd, Croydon, CR0 4YY
US: Printed and bound by Thomson-Shore, 7300 West Joy Road, Dexter, MI 48130

We operate a distinctive and ethical publishing philosophy in
all areas of our business, from our global network of authors to
production and worldwide distribution.

Contents

We were going to dedicate this to named family members but they strenuously and unpleasantly resisted the proposal as they hate academies. Therefore, next best, our hearty thanks and admiration to those ground-breaking entrepreneurs who are pushing the boundaries of educational thought, rejecting the restraints of old-fashioned ideas of service and engaging with opportunities and innovations, nationally and globally, that will be our 'futureshock', from which there is no way back. Normal family relations may resume at some time in the future.

Acknowledgements

We would like to thank the following for their comments and encouragement, their various inputs and examples and the continued energy they show in resisting the privatisation and financialisation of England's education system. Janet Downs of *Local Schools Network* and Warwick Mansell's *Education Uncovered* have been sources of great value. Material from the Anti Academies Alliance (AAA) and the Campaign for State Education (CASE) have fed ideas, evidence and argument.

Youssef El-Gingihy wrote *How to Dismantle the NHS in 10 Easy Steps* and it was hearing him speak and reading the book that inspired the authors to write a parallel book about a similar privatisation development looming large in the school sector in England. We thank him for not minding that we ripped off his title.

The local John Roan Resists cadre have been an inspiration, frightening in their efforts to retain their secondary school as a local resource, as the founder in the 1600s would have surely wished. The parents, teachers, teaching assistants and ancillary staff of Sherington School, London SE7 who fought a magnificent campaign to successfully resist a plot to join a large academy chain. Local resistance groups country-wide are inspirational and show why we should not give up working to keep schools in the public, democratically accountable sector.

On a more direct level, Sanita Edwards has been tireless in inputting Terry's text and Gillian Fairbanks has corrected and re-corrected hastily amassed versions.

David Ewens, John Galloway and Tom Mann endured the complete draft and commented wisely.

Sue Allen, George Hudson, Harvey Morris and Stephen Steadman were insightful and provocative in their reactions to an early draft.

Preface

This is a short book, written in anger, but with vestiges of hope still afloat despite this current miasmic 2019 sewer of government social policy which disregards social responsibility while making rich friends richer, more powerful and more self-satisfied. The book could have been written 10 years ago when we were, under a Labour government, already sliding towards the sludge of 'every "man" for himself' and the 'let's-pretend-we-care-but-we really-don't' world. However, now our children's state education is being remorselessly degraded.

So, a bitter book about education because there is much to be bitter about. We attempt to show with scorn and irony the template being enacted to destabilise, diminish and dismantle a system, wrest it away from any sense of democratic control and impoverish the experience of childhood. The collusion and deceit were already in place, the guidance has been enacted and schools are lost in a wilderness of confusion that now characterises the second most important developmental institution for children; the first being the family.

Inspired by the deepest, covert thoughts of the fiercest privatisers are beliefs that public services in public ownership and control are mismanaged and that state finances are there to be plundered. Who makes the connection between high salaries for senior leaders and reduced funds available for classrooms and the children in them? Who spots the myriad, over-priced services contracted out in this era of freedom? Who recognises the staffing cuts, governance changes and curriculum contraction? This will continue and expand further until we reclaim our schools!

The ugly situation we describe and mock-advocacy presented emerge from two retirees who have 'seen it all', voyeurs who remain happily, pathetically optimistic and even accept that

1

some head teachers and some multi-academy trusts are worthy. Indeed some of our best friends work in them. It is *the system* which is poisonous: it drives people to behave in ways which do not accord with their values, runs counter to what we value about childhood and development and is responsive to a troubling immorality in terms of care for people, damage to the young and misuse of public money!

1. Embrace the third way

Introduction

The new educational world order is marked by a parting of the ways. Once services for the people were designed, financed and managed by public bodies. Our representatives, elected by the people, locally and nationally, were in charge and responsible for spending the country's tax receipts for the benefit of all – NHS, education, defence, social services for young and old, criminal justice, transport, power and other infrastructure elements from roads to postal services. Put simply, this is the *first way*, comfortable, secure and homely. For many, it was the best way, the only way. But it did not make a profit! On the other side was private enterprise, which the nation concedes has a legitimate place in the economy with shareholders, profits and astronomic salaries for some. This is the *second way*. The *third way* is that co-operative, balanced sharing between the state and the private sector, with the state doing what it is good at (very little, some argue) and private enterprise, with all its energy, creativity and value-for-money, contributing its strengths. That balanced relationship has not remained strong and stable with many state institutions slipping ever more out of the deadening bureaucratic blundering that was central government or local authority control into fully private hands.

The third way is a globalised financial and business environment linking with governments for 'progress' and profit, especially profit. It operates in both the making of things and the delivery of services. Education is one part of a larger whole, just one high-cost state function which private enterprise has successfully muscled in on. To scrutinise the ecology of schools and education, we need to spread the net wide at the outset or it would be difficult to understand how something so startlingly, transformatively crazy could be happening to our children's schools. The neo-liberal, third-way macroeconomics that governments thought they were buying into has opened up for business an education system, in place and maturing since 1944, but said to have lost its way, and which now requires entrepreneurs to bring it back on course for the twenty-first century. Education has been a national, state-controlled, democratically accessible system with 'ethically sound', 'uplifting goals' of care for all, responsive and child friendly. The cunningly contrived message is that wiser heads should now prevail. The case has been made that things had got soppy and sloppy and the nation is fortunate to have clever, energetic people who can put education back on track and, incidentally, make a lot of money on the side. The sub-contracting of education, to what are unashamedly private enterprises, has salvaged the system from dire decline and swept away all this social, equity and welfare nonsense. The new regime has got us back to a focussed, assessment-based

The ten easy steps to dismantle the education system

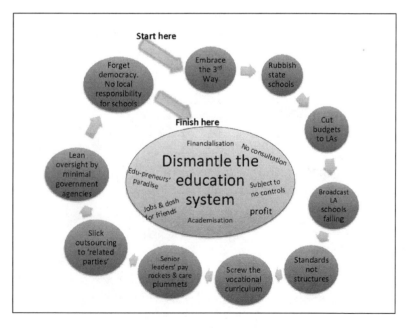

hierarchical curriculum with a teacher workforce that actually *works* for us and serious, disciplined, hard-working pupils who know their place. There will always be those nay-sayers, those who talk of the new regime offering a joyless, down-trodden, repressive, dispiriting experience for pupils and staff alike, but they can be faced down – or, more likely, ignored utterly.

The way is clear and the 10 steps are tested, fool-proof and ongoing. 'Embrace': how can that be bad? 'The third way': surely a good thing, progress beyond the tensions between government control and private enterprise. The privatisers in the ascendancy will brush aside the trivial claims that this is a system given over to the ruthless, scandalous clutches of voracious, amoral, commercial plundering. The coup is pretty well complete. Just watch the *Blob* (Michael Gove's term when Education Secretary), the 'intellectuals', 'experts', lefties and luvvies from whence comes the faux dismay at what they are doing.

Neo-liberalism

'Neo' is good and so is 'liberalism', so what can go wrong? Conservative thinkers have snatched the language, burnished it and made it their own. The mantra of 'freedom', opposite to captivity and restriction, is good and could never be seen as out of control and beyond reasonable regulation. The 'third way' was the label given to private-public partnerships. It has not turned out to be a balanced partnership, but a sell-out, a buy-out and all the better profits for that.

By the late 1990s, the third way was an established, respectable attitude, an ideology and a relationship. It was about the government and private enterprise working together paid for by taxes. The government thought it could control the terms of the relationship and ensure that the supposed drive and innovation of capital could be harnessed to socialist, or at least socially responsible, state provision. Some dreamt of an even-handed, centrism, reconciling right and left political wings, a heavenly synthesis. They reckoned without the slyness, greed and tenacity of the business mentality and the ability of private enterprise to make alliances with the powerful and emasculate the weak local political controllers and the even weaker professional lobby. Some might say that, in 2019, the UK has arrived at a selfishness and austerity, resulting from investment capitalism let off the leash, allowing services for the people to be stripped bare and made mean and the needy blamed for their plight. Some say we are still heading downhill. They don't know that there is even more deregulation in prospect, more assets to be stripped and there are some who just can't wait. Get used to it.

The *Blob*, as Michael Gove, then Education Secretary described so-called education professionals and academics, might get angry. The Blob, even focussing just on education, are mad enough to want to dig up dirt on how the 'crime' against the people is being committed, claiming that private enterprise works on the basis of profit, rake-off, shareholder bonanza, top-whack salaries for chief executives and cronies and that its prime concern is not the public good. The new breed say that is not so. But for private enterprise, from building firms to healthcare providers, drawing on public money to do new work is a dream opportunity they would be foolish not to grasp. The new organisations are fronted by well-mannered, polite people with good diction and dress sense who can fool them all – government departments, local authorities and charities – into thinking that they are truly in it for the good of the people, though it would be naive to think that was their primary objective. It has been necessary to undermine and devalue the principles and practices of social provision for the people set up long ago. A listing could be made of the public utilities sold off (water, power, transport, telecommunications), the building partnerships under public, private initiatives (PPI), health provision, prison and probation management (oops, see later), accommodation for the elderly and others with social care needs. But we won't. Our focus is on school education. It is true there are instances of chaos and rip-offs elsewhere in the commercial world, which are becoming obvious. Some of the same may be happening in the new regime in provision for our children, but this can be tolerated if the overall picture is good and getting brighter.

Ronald Reagan, as American president, convincingly claimed that, 'The nine most terrifying words in the English language are, "I'm from the government and I'm here to help"[1].' That got a lot of coverage and the riposte to it has always seemed po-faced and limp-wristed. 'Well the government takes our taxes to provide us with all those good things like education, and health, builds roads and even ensures poor people don't suffer too much...blah, blah, blah.'

Public services privatised

Let the private sector in with limited regulation and see how creatively firms diversify way beyond their core businesses and expertise. *Virgin* moved into health, having started with record stores, then planes then trains. *Interserve* moved on from construction and support services into welfare-to-work, providing training and development for job-seekers, probation services as well as public finance initiative deals with hospitals and schools. *Capita*, billed as a 'business process outsourcing' outfit, won NHS contracts for administrative services, locum doctors and set up something called Primary Care Support for GP practices, pharmacies, dentists and opticians. *Serco* moved imaginatively from origins in RCA Records (owned by Sony Music) to operating in health, transport, justice, and immigration.

Carillion was a multinational facilities management and construction company and, though it successfully acquired loads of government contracts, it stuck to its core business. Mostly. Until it crashed spectacularly.

Babcock was into complex engineering projects which meant a lot of Ministry of Defence work, but it could spread its interest to education and now Babcock Education bills itself as 'the largest integrated education improvement and support services provider in the UK'.

They might call it a rapacious move to grasp government money at all costs but lessons have been learnt from which others moving into the field might benefit. Firstly, you do not need sector-specific expertise, except in winning bids which often means under-cutting in-house providers (in healthcare, for instance), dressing up your own capabilities beyond any track record and bungling through. It is notable how organisations 'slip' from being not-for-profits, sometimes from management or employee buyouts, into just plain private companies with shareholders and chief execs on enormous salaries. So Capita came out of CIPFA (Chartered Institute of Public Finance) and Babcock bought the *Surrey School Support Services* (4S) after it became an employee buy-out and is now on-line as *Babcock 4S*. Additionally, there are acquisitions where a larger firm gets into a new business by buying a small organisation already in the field. Tricky, but if you know business and have got the nerve, you can go far.

Scandals have been commonplace, often involving huge amounts of public money. Capita has had its share of these, but at a turnover of £3,900M, pre-tax profits of £272M and chief executive Jon Lewis (appointed 2017) on £725,000 per annum fixed for 3 years plus a maximum bonus of £1.45M and long-term share payments of £2.2M, questions might well be raised about whether public money should be syphoned off like this. But that's business.

The interlocking of firms hunting out government money find it useful to limit their external competitors. Rigging tendering arrangements so that they suit private enterprise is important, especially if it puts the in-house team on the back foot. The NHS published guidance on 'Any Qualified Provider' which made the bold claim to be 'extending patient choice' and 'liberating the

NHS', so that Clinical Commissioning Groups as part of Primary Care Trusts should identify services to out-source[2]. This threw the door wide open to competition (another word that can't be bad). In-house services, usually the current providers, could also bid, but they too often do not have the same bidding skills and, if the bidding procedures can be faulted, as they were when Richard Branson's Virgin Care lost a bid, the NHS must pay out a large sum. In this example, Virgin did not get an £82M contract in Surrey. It went to a cuddly local consortium made up of Surrey Health, Children and Families Service partnered by the local hospital, a local partnership trust and two local social enterprises. In an out of court settlement Branson got £320,000 for his trouble, and quite right too! People got up in arms about that, with public money allocated to a cash-strapped NHS trust going to a millionaire just to avoid a court case that might have cost more. People should not whine about these things. It's business!

Companies find that it is handy to get auditors onside as Carillion did, albeit too late. KPMG did not blow the whistle on this business and, at a government enquiry where these auditors were interrogated about their role, an MP joked that he 'would not hire you to do an audit of the contents of my fridge'. To be frank, who would want to audit Labour MP Peter Kyle's fridge? And who cares what he and his committee think? They are toothless. It's business.

In the bigger picture of 'rigging', getting the right friends and slipping carefully from a publicly-owned concern to a not-for-profit to a fully private enterprise we should look without shame or envy at top people's pay and other rewards. Capita's boss is doing well, Branson, living off-shore is doing better still and the Persimmon boss got a £75M bonus, because the firm had not put a cap on the possible share bonus, and had done extremely well out of house sales cushioned by the input from the government's 'affordable homes scheme'. This is all part of the brakes off, no holds barred, private enterprise free for all where, shock-horror, 3567 UK bankers 'earned' over €1M in 2016/17. To top it all, we/ they can fail horribly, laughably and still walk off with a stash of loot, as Fred Goodwin of RBS notoriously did, even though he accepted a reduction in his pension to £342,000 per year! Call it 'corporate looting' if you like, but it is how business works. And to top it all *even more*, there are the PFIs, Private Finance Initiatives, which show prolific gains for builders and developers. Even the National Audit Office reported to the Commons Public Accounts Committee[3] how these deals, on reflection, had been bad for the public purse. Why shouldn't taxpayers pay nearly £200bn to contractors under private finance deals for at least 25 years, even if they are 40 per cent more expensive than using public money? Enormous amounts have gone on NHS projects, entailing continuing servicing. A total of £4.8bn will have gone from school budgets by 2020. In eight local authorities, schools will pay £252M in interest over the next 2 to 5 years, in payments which are ring-fenced and cannot be reduced. PFIs abound. This is not a *scandal* – that would be unfair, though it is certainly an expensive and enduring debt placed on that public purse, noticeable in school buildings as in hospitals. The *PFI 'heist'* was all so cleverly negotiated by privatisers in establishing the advantageous terms of deals that ensured that in the long term they extracted more wealth than they could previously have dreamt of[4]. It has not exactly back-fired and the result has not been huge criticism, sackings, court cases or a significant change of direction – except fewer PFI deals contracted – and no one who was made rich has subsequently been made poorer. That's business, business out of control of state regulation. This third way business approach allowed the Labour government, from 1998 onwards, to build schools, hospitals and other capital projects without the need to raise taxes to pay for them, which is always unpopular. That was the perfect example of government and business working together[5]. *That was the deal!*

What we learn from operations in the corporate world are the following:

- Have friends in high places (politicians and others) who create laws which let you in;
- Get the public onside;
- Establish regulations to give private operators an advantage;
- Ensure that other regulators are swept away or weakened;
- Creep in carefully and seem benign;
- Nurture collusion between understaffed and underpowered regulators and private operators;
- Let salary levels rocket for upper echelons and bear down on trade unions and staff;
- Get a seat at the 'top table' to talk to and 'advise' national policy makers;
- Work at polished publicity: branding and mottos work a treat in kidding the public and politicians alike.

This happens to organisations, big and small, public utilities and local amenities. A small shock/horror by comparison with events in the wider world is the story of Hastings Pier, a public amenity. Built in 1886, it burnt down twice and was rebuilt twice. In 2017, it won the RIBA Stirling Prize for architecture for a rebuild, received £13M from the Heritage Lottery, further funds from shares bought by locals and another half million from a crowd-funded community effort. Despite all this, it went into administration and was sold for a pittance to an entrepreneur, a dodgy entrepreneur with other businesses going into liquidation owing thousands to HMRC and others and had county court judgements against his companies. Locals questioned whether a private owner would safeguard the public interest. He did not. It remained locked for months. Again, that's business. A local volunteer lamented this community asset passing into private hands and saw it as 'a bereavement'. On its reopening in 2019, it was to have none of the culturally uplifting events and attractions which people thought the expense and award-winning architecture deserved, but if it is not going to make money, no owner would do more and the people of Hastings should think themselves lucky to have got the pier open at all, thanks to an entrepreneur, 'dodgy' or not. Years ago, one of the authors slept under that pier on a summer night with friends. That opportunity remains, but such sentimentality gets us nowhere. Other people sleep there now, not from choice, but that is another story that we must harden our hearts to.

Education: a billion-pound business for sale

On to education, a billion-pound business which companies have been sniffing around for 2 decades and into which, by 2019, they have made huge inroads. There is much to be learnt from how private enterprise works in other sectors, as mentioned above, and these skills have transferred well to education. Planned public spending in the UK in 2020 amounts to over £800bn, 18 per cent going to healthcare and 10 per cent, or £87.7 billion, to education at all levels[6]. That is a very attractive trough to get into.

Currently, testing in education and much school literature is supplied by the Pearson Group. Capita owns SIMS (School Information Management System). Babcocks, once builders and machine makers, run training and school improvement. The Education Endowment Foundation (EEF), a charity in little more than name, is bringing in big government grants for essentially conservative education projects like *Challenge the Gap*[7] (reducing low attainment amongst disadvantaged groups), which did not work, but, hey, good for them for trying. Never a thought to simply reducing child poverty – and why would they, where is the profit in that?

Groups, which are in essence businesses registered as

charities, have 'won' contracts worth millions for work, which could easily have been, and indeed was, run in-house in the service of the country's children. Examination boards are one example, but mergers and closures have led to only five examination boards remaining and, sensibly, most have set themselves up as charities, just like public schools, as any wise financial advisor would recommend.

GL Assessment used to be NFER Nelson (turnover £28M in 2017) with a reported profit of £10M and two directors together share £854,000. *AQA*, motto 'Realising potential', had 11 in the executive team earning over £120,000.

That is small fry compared to *Pearson* with a global turnover of £4,500M and a chief executive with a pay package of £1.5M in 2017. The examination arm is Edexel. Pearson, as a multinational, does not pretend to be a charity. It is a big beast in the field, and in 2015 decided to focus 100 per cent on education; that is how attractive that market is. Pearson has even set up its own college in London. Hats off to Pearson, even if it made a loss in 2018 and was criticised for having too much influence in government circles as well as having parts of its business registered off-shore. Influence politicians and minimise taxes is what they do.

Edu-business has been a big expansion area and is a long-overdue recognition by government that it is no good at running services. Sad, but true, and it will not be long before France, Germany, Holland, Denmark and so on will understand that truth and go the way of England, following hard on the heels of the USA, the world's most successful economy.

Academies: the big deal

On to *academies*, each a limited company, converted from standard local authority schools and placed in multi-academy trusts (MATs), or opening as free schools with still 10,000 further schools (2019 numbers) ripe for picking off and taking into the private sector. There are 240 MATs running primary schools (36 per cent) and 85 running secondary schools (72 per cent of the total)[8]. If the schools budget in 2017-18 was nearly £42bn, then half goes directly from government, via the Education and Skills Funding Agency (ESFA), to academies or MATs, bypassing local authorities.

This started reassuringly enough in the early stages of 'the third way' with city academies, delightfully, if naively, prompted by Blair's centrist, sharing, big-tent way of getting private capital involved as partners. Schools in trouble which the LA was not managing to improve were the focus. These academies were sponsored by a philanthropist and central and local government were quite relaxed about this, even excited at the innovative potential as laid out in the Learning and Skills Act 2000[9]. In 2010, the policy was turned on its head so that any school judged satisfactory or better could apply to become an academy (2010 Academies Act). In time, the Secretary of State for Education extended the policy (Education and Adoption Act, 2016) to force local authority schools which Ofsted judged 'inadequate' to become academies within a MAT. MATs were given the task of improving the school, a function earlier carried out by LAs.

Thousands of schools have become academies, with necessary disregard for teachers' and teaching assistants' conditions of service and job losses mounting, beyond what one might have expected with the education cuts, but we still sail on. There may be NO convincing, robust evidence yet to show academies perform better whether they are of the conversion or sponsored (many forced) variety. But they do have better branding and they know how to get the grants. They are favoured. Look at the discretionary payments made over the last 3 years. The biggest losers have been the local authorities along with the much-vaunted democratic mandate they had to safeguard local children's education. The biggest winners have been the chief executives and senior staff in MATs and academy head teachers, indubitably better equipped to guarantee best educational values and high standards.

The official head teacher pay scale, as set out by the DfE in 2018, is pretty generous. In the tiniest country primary, a head just starting out would be on £45,000. In the largest Inner London secondary schools, salaries could come close to £120,000. The academy pay-world is altogether different:

- In 2015-16, in 91 MATs, there were 1076 people paid between £100,000 and £150,000.
- A total of 87 Trust chief executives were on over £150,000.
- Harris Federation chief Sir Daniel Moynihan was earning over £400,000.
- It cannot be repeated enough, that to get the best people and the best performance you have to pay well. Sir Dan earns every penny of that salary, as Lord Harris himself confirms.

The *Academies Enterprise Trust* with 60 schools (33,000 children) has 62 people in the £100,000+ pay bracket and three earning over £150,000[10]. Established innocuously in 2008 by the friendly-sounding Greensward Charitable Trust, and with the strap-line 'Inspiring each and every child to choose a remarkable life' (original underlining), the trust has certainly claimed for itself 'remarkable' salaries.

United Learning Trust, 'The best in everyone', has 70 schools and the chief executive, Jon Coles, had a salary of £160,000 in 2016/17 rising to £240,000 in 2017/18, which can only be because he does an exceptional job of educational leadership. Accounts show that 19 others in the trust are paid over £100,000. Core values are listed as 'Ambition, confidence, creativity, respect, enthusiasm, determination' and many of these are evident in its ability to acquire additional grants from the DfE, wisely only available to the academy sector (£685,674 to stabilise its finances in 2016/17) and to have large debts written off before taking over academies in trouble under other management (£245,000 received for each of the Richard Rose academies taken over in 2013/14). It seems a favoured MAT, receiving grants from the Strategic School Improvement Fund, and can still get into a spat with the department about predicted school numbers on the basis of which annual funding is calculated. The DfE does not like over-estimates. Coles plays hardball, as you would expect from an ex-DfE senior civil servant, sending a stern email:

> dismayed that the Department is proposing unilaterally to breach its contract with us...Department/EFA has no arguable case...stance you are taking is lawful...grateful for your confirmation within the next 24 hours that the EFA will honour the government's contract with us and fund us on the estimates basis set out in our funding agreement, so that this dispute does not escalate further[11].

Firm stuff.

The impressive **Harris Federation**, 'Educating 32,000 pupils in 47 highly successful academies in and around London', has its own annual conference, offers its own teacher training and claims that, 'Every Harris Academy inspected so far has been judged to be "Good" or "Outstanding".' The ethos is expressed as 'Excel, Exceed, Explore' (Chafford Hundred) or 'Excellence, Respect, Integrity, Innovation, Collaboration, Trust' (Chobham) or 'Courage, Challenge and Success' (Morden).

Well done *Ark*, with 38 schools and 35 staff on salaries of £100–150K with the CEO one of the 87 earning over £150,000. Its ethos has six pillars: 'high expectations, excellent teaching, knowing every child, depth for breadth, exemplary behaviour and always learning'. Elsewhere, Ark Multi Academy Trust states: 'Our driving principles are Excellence, Citizenship,

Participation, Persistence'. Some individual schools have a board of governors to die for: Ark Greenwich Free School ('Ambition, Growth, Fellowship, Scholarship') has a chair who was Head of the Education Unit at Policy Exchange (think tank), often in the media, previously in the Cabinet Office and one-time Head of Education in the Prime Minister's Strategy Unit under both Brown and Cameron. Another governor is a solicitor at an international law firm, another a partner at McKinsey & Co and another on the staff at Eton. There is also a trained Ofsted inspector in the mix. Ark has projects in India and Uganda which are looking at ways to 'improve school quality and student performance', and in Kenya and South Africa, where 'they are developing low-cost school information systems to drive student progress'. Very laudable. Ark was formerly ARK (Absolute Returns for Kids – a Christian organisation), a charity formed in 2002 by a group of businessmen. There was some change of status in 2014 which defies understanding for some, but its *UK Education* line in the 2016 accounts gives a total of £11,874,000, with whatever the *Educational Partnership Group* means given as £2,765,000. Presumably this is all the management, oversight and chief executive expenditure. This is the sort of funding that would previously have been in the hands of the LA and have been squandered.

You cannot beat them on the dream-up-a-good-ethos/motto/strap-line. The websites are phenomenally impressive, displaying no false modesty. They get high-profile names in and then quote the good things they say about the school. Good business. All this comes at a price because public relations and managing the customer-facing literature and media exposure does not come cheap. One could speculate that all this takes close to 10 per cent of the budget which is money and effort not directed at the children. But that is business. Local authorities top-sliced as little as 0.9 per cent from the schools' budget (Schools Forum agreement, Greenwich, London).

It is not necessary to be in a MAT to earn big money: 29 single school academy trusts have chief executives, in effect the head teachers, earning over £150K and 13 of these are reportedly facing financial difficulties[16].

The statement has to be made again and again that there is no connection between high salaries for top people and getting into financial difficulties. Nor can it be shown that redundancies of teaching assistants or deleting some frivolous, creative subjects from the school timetable are connected in any way at all with those justifiably huge salaries.

Inspection teams, teacher development, legal advice, accountancy services

This entire field is opened up to quasi-private organisations – academies – in receipt of a large portion of the government spend on schools, for buying in services, most of which were previously supplied by the local authority. The local authority used to retain a portion of the funding allocated for schools to provide services ranging from caretaking and dinners, repairs and 'additional space', wages and human resources. This has been slashed with the numbers directly employed by local councils reduced by 60 per cent. The claim has been they did not do a good job and were not 'value-for-money'. There is obviously everything to play for in managing the schools and all the ancillary services. The edu-preneurs are scheming hard on multiple levels to maximise their take. This is about incentives, and the belief that people work harder, faster and to a higher standard when there are bonuses and perks. Private works; public does not. Reagan had it right. What is being done is all for the benefit of the children, and embracing the third way, a paradise for CEOs, managers and bureaucrats has the spin-off that students also get the best. This is a promise.

2. Rubbish the management of state schools

Introduction

Here is what you do, if you want to remove a system from public ownership, control and responsibility. The first step is to question and undermine what is going on in that system, with the effect that all stakeholders come to expect change. This might be described as a 'softening up' strategy. It is best to do this through public criticism of attainment levels. That way your position is projected as honest and transparent. Even if attainment is going up year by year, as judged by the testing imposed on schools, it is possible to give the figures a negative spin, and that, together with accounts of bad behaviour in classrooms and violence in and outside schools, is helpful. Target teachers as 'not up to the job', label them inadequate at every possible opportunity and belittle teacher education. After all, any competent adult and specialists in their own fields can do the job of teaching. While you're doing that, it will be legitimate and popular to cut the funding to universities, which allegedly 'train' teachers, adding the even more popular proposal that cash saved can be invested directly at the 'chalkface'. Introduce changes in the curriculum, but do not bother to consult with those who would supposedly know best. The curriculum is not an area that excites much interest anyway and you are taking advantage of the country's justified fatigue with the contributions of experts, the Blob, as Michael Gove called them.

Escalate resolutely

The advice is to start small, as with the early academies (2000–10), or 'offer to help out' with staff development, assessment systems etc. But you have to grow. Do not be timid. Hack at the system from the top and destroy or sideline any opposition. Eviscerate teacher unions, limit conversations with them and certainly stop short of 'consultation'. Make a national curriculum loose enough for your purposes, consult few people and do it quickly. Make sure that it is not the teachers' curriculum.

Criticise attainment levels

Promote public unrest and undermine schools with jibes that they are not doing the job well enough, that teachers are not competent or they are concerned too much with enjoyment of learning or project-based nonsense or following up children's interests. Point out other countries that are doing better at the regular international measures of attainment (see later). Pay particular attention to 'the achievement gap'. This is the performance of poorer pupils compared with others – essentially the 17 per cent on free school meals – and commit to solving that. Hammer absolutely any curriculum area where there are statistical measures that show poor current performance across the system. Reading levels are a good example. Promise that academies will do better.

Control regulatory agents

Turn Her Majesty's Inspectorate into a hit squad. Go further and set up something less kind and forgiving than the old HMI and get them out there judging standards. What is more, publish results. Go the whole hog and while keeping tabs on Ofsted, the 'scorched earth' Office for Standards in Education, subcontract out the work to teams, training them up to inspect according to *The Handbook*. Ofsted can be used as the tool for protecting academies and for forcing schools to become academies when they are judged 'inadequate'.

Behaviour is bad

Push on and make a fuss about bad behaviour, undermine teacher education institutions and press for more discipline. Everything and anything bad can be registered as the fault of schools. Knife crime to teenage pregnancies are things that 'schools are not doing enough to prevent'. Just read *Getting the Buggers to Behave*[13] and devise an ambitious behaviour and discipline policy. Getting tough on discipline, adding zero tolerance and standing resolute about the place of exclusions will all win support. Continue by linking behaviour with attainment and attack current standards which are inevitably not high enough, especially when compared with other countries, and set benchmarks. Then publish results school by school and local authority by local authority to prove your point. Naming and shaming is just and we know it works. Academies can flaunt their policies of zero tolerance as a solution. Be fierce, be uncompromising and be strong because these characteristics are rightly admired.

Privatise support services

THEN, while your mates in the city have screwed up, forcing government to bail them out, go for austerity in public services, cut funding and expect teachers to work harder and even bring out accountants who reason that schools can do even more with even less[14]. Schools, used to working with local authority services, from counselling to youth work, must be shown the error of their ways. These services will be cheaper now in the privatised sector, especially as they reduce to a hardly detectable presence in the absence of realistic funding. Be expansive and adventurous with spending on non-staff items from the private sector (more on this later).

Freedom has to be good

The BIG idea was to 'free' schools, to take funding from LAs and give the work to some people who would do the job better, more responsibly and more effectively. This policy began in a small way in 2001 with the creation of city academies which were 'failing schools', ones which local authorities seemed unable to raise up, almost always in areas of deprivation (get the connection). The obvious solution was to bring in a private sponsor while sidelining the LA, but at that time it was with the agreement of the LA. From Labour's good idea for saving failing schools in 2001 (thank you Andrew Adonis, guru architect of the city academy scheme), the later development of academies, 2010 onwards, was about good schools converting and incentivised (bribed?) into becoming academies and thus moving out of LA control. Yet another clever move by entrepreneurs where a policy is reinvented to serve completely different purposes and put LAs 'out of business'. That opens the door wide for an alternative structure, firstly a quasi-market and then a proper business structure. What speed of change; what emerging opportunities.

Training or education of teachers is not needed

Teacher training was an overblown luxury. Child development, pah! Structures of knowledge, who needs them? Pedagogic skills, what's so sophisticated about them? Schools are places we have all been to, we know all about them, we know what good teachers are like and you don't need to train them; they can just learn alongside others who have been doing the job for years.

Curriculum does not need consultation with experts

Experts are unnecessary. What we learn in schools, how we learn it and assess it is obvious. What a waste of good money it would be to gather together historians, from the highest reaches of academia to secondary and primary enthusiasts for the subject, to pay them to sketch out the curriculum, have it trialled and improved and adapted in different areas. Why do that when a few chosen people supported by the brightest, inexperienced souls from the Cabinet Office or elsewhere in the depleted corridors of educational power could knock together something quite adequate? Do the same for maths and English, science too, but that may, at secondary level, have remained in the grasp of actual scientists. This is because those brightest of the bright recruited to civil service positions are Oxbridge arts buffs and cannot knock out a science curriculum better than the existing one. You win some, you lose some. Fortunately, unless used as alternative soft option subjects for students failing in our revitalised core curriculum, art, drama, music and dance – hobbies really – can be 'squeezed' or eliminated for whole year groups.

Divide and rule and undermine

Take staffing in schools by the scruff. Consider the case of an experienced and enthusiastic head of department, called in to the head's office and informed that, although the GCSE results had again improved, 'capability procedures' were being put in place because the results did not match the tracking predictions projected for that cohort. Ignore any *excuses* of a new syllabus, introduced without agreement, or the department's results following a national trend. Someone had taken their eye off the ball. Necessary outcome: one-time successful and dedicated teacher aggrieved, angry and looking to leave the profession. You are only as good as your most recent results This could never be seen as deliberate policy to undermine a teacher's professionalism and sense of worth or to force him/her out. In this case the teacher whined to the head that, for the previous 3 years, the school felt unable to employ a permanent subject-qualified second-in-department because of financial restraints. Ignore this and ignore the cheeky riposte that the school's budget seemed well able to support an ever-increasing layer of expensive senior managers, with little experience, to facilitate the 'capability' process being applied[15]. Welcome to the new era where staff will not dress casually but will look like bank managers or estate agents and ensure they are wearing their lanyards at all times – the academy owns them.

Assess them til the pips squeak

Teacher appraisal, if done with vigour – and how else would

you do it if the drive for improvement is to become the norm? – divides, of course it does: sheep and goats, good and bad, toughies and wimps. No longer allow staff to feel that teaching is a co-operative endeavour, discourage staff support and promote a competitive and judgemental environment where everyone is looking out for themselves and encouraged to pass judgement on their colleagues. Result: teachers will leave the profession in droves and younger, cheaper staff can be employed who are more compliant and less of the mind that education is being replaced by exam-factory systems to produce less rounded, articulate citizens. Perhaps fewer new recruits coming in and increased numbers leaving after a very few years 'because it is a crap job' is a bit of a problem. A Nation Education Union report finds one in five teachers expect to leave in 2 years and a quarter of newly qualified teachers expect to leave within 5 years[16].

Remember, undermining starts at the top with head teachers employed on fixed-term contracts where renewal is determined by exam results and Ofsted requirements that are used to create an atmosphere of fear. Fight any desire to lift the spirits and commitment of teachers and encourage the development of creative and confident children! Who wants that? Discourage individual discovery and replace it with a system that narrows school experience to a pass/fail challenge in an increasingly constrained curriculum, assessed largely by end of course written examinations, even if these do not suit everyone. Edge out creativity and enquiry, even if the creative industries are near the top of Britain's GDP producers. Remember education *is* a business and business likes quick financial gains.

Only wimps and lefties want a return to old-style 'education'. Dismiss calls for teachers to be respected and treated as so-called 'professionals'. No sensible authority today thinks we can afford teacher education that incorporates an understanding of the history, philosophy and psychology of education. Resist any move away from simply 'training' on the job and reduce learning to the techniques that will fulfil a school's need to compete with its neighbours and display 'outstanding' on the school gates. What can possibly be wrong with that?' It's an educational philosophy wrapped in good business sense.

Fortunately, a national inspection regime was created to replace local authority supervision, which was judged to be too kindly and matey, and gradually a competitive and less co-operative atmosphere amongst local schools gained ground. Step by step, Ofsted created a super-efficient, one-size-fits-all format for judging effective teaching to which teachers could conform or fail, despite years of 'successful' experience. This new system is uniform and could be criticised for inconsistent reporting or alienating staff and pupils but where is the evidence that it is contributing to serious mental health problems in both? If heads and classroom teachers try to continue with a 'child-centred' curriculum the pressure of league tables and the 'fear' of Ofsted will surely make resistance increasingly difficult. It has become rare for professionals to be confident or foolhardy enough to openly question the diktats from on high. At last, the teachers have been brought to heel. Why did it take so long?

Ignore the Blob which says Ofsted should be replaced with a new organisation based on the premise that schools are staffed with professionals who are open to advice but who need support and encouragement from a constructive inspection regime that is prepared to speak truth to governments about resources, staff training, workloads and facilities, as well as being there to investigate reported lapses in standards in institutions and individuals and with the resources to improve them. What a load of baloney! Few suggest that inspections are unnecessary and if the current organisation is perceived as assuming most teachers are inadequate, that's fair enough. Setting out a specific format for lesson planning and delivery by Ofsted could never be construed as undermining imaginative and innovative teaching and teachers who don't conform. These are ones who might be remembered by pupils and parents as being 'different' and 'inspirational' but are now forced to take early retirement because this maverick behaviour has no place. They are the natural wastage any business has to contend with.

Ofsted is here to stay and the academy sector can work with it, and, indeed, must. Ofsted does not always get it right and we can live with the anecdotes of inspectors in the wrong lessons (Question: 'Why is there so much drama going on?' Response: 'Because it's a drama lesson.' Inspector: 'Oops, meant to be in English.'); inspectors who could not hack it in the classroom turning up as inspectors; and the inspector who reported that asking a pupil at the end of a lesson what they have learnt, and the absence of a clear and precise answer, meant that teacher and lesson had failed.

Some might say Ofsted is not fit for purpose, but fail and schools' reputations and teachers' careers are 'on-the-line'. However, if you can pull the wool over their eyes (they are not that bright) then you (the academy) can come out with an (undeserved) 'good' judgement.

It is intelligent to see Ofsted as a regulatory agent academies can do business with and many of their decisions are to the advantage of the academy sector. The experience of inspection may be no more unpleasant than for teachers in any other school, but teach to the test, run a tight discipline ship, brief teachers so that they have the right answers and all will be well.

Inspection is part of the architecture of the education system in England and, to be successful, you have to work with it, and work it to your advantage. Judgements placing schools in special measures mean an academy order and another school for a MAT to take over. If an academy is in trouble over an inspection judgement, unlike with local authority schools, there are ways to negotiate the time allowed to improve the school, two or three or even four monitoring visits before they (Ofsted and ESFA and RSC) would start the process of handing over to another MAT. The David Ross Education Trust (DRET mission: 'to give every child attending one of our schools a world class education') has four Ofsted visits to improve Lodge Park Academy in Derby (motto: 'Broadening Horizons'), criticised for 'mundane teaching'. This is a pre-termination warning notice and threatens to end the academy's funding agreement. The academies sector has this covered and the promise of 'rapid and sustained improvement' is a challenge that can be met. It is always helpful to be able to negotiate behind the scenes for a sensible improvement timetable that will work for us. It is letting the side down if 'orphan' schools like Sedgehill in south-east London are not taken over by a MAT sponsor because complications like PFI agreements make it unprofitable.

Competition not co-operation

Always remember that competition is healthy, whether the school sports day or the academic ranking of pupils, from infant classrooms right up to the Olympics. It is a good thing. After a long, dark period of encouraging mutual support and co-operation in, and between, schools (London Challenge and all that), there has been a great leap forward with the introduction of academies and 'free' schools that increasingly result in the long-overdue annihilation of local education authorities and the services they claimed to provide. Budgets decrease. Academies in MATs are unable to spend time and resources supporting neighbouring schools easily as MATs operate across large geographic areas and these organisations may have little understanding of the communities they serve. This could be seen as a challenge for the academy sector, but the creativity and energy released by being free of local control will amply make up for any perceived drawback. Great schools in super-MATs can collaborate, overcoming geography and achieving the best. That is what we say and that is what we do. Apparent co-operation does come in handy in generously helping a school that has failed its Ofsted and received an academy order. Such help is a useful prelude to a takeover, enhancing a particular MAT's likelihood to be assigned as the sponsor. A cunning plan but a just reward.

The competitive world of education means you have to push to the limits, push staff, push pupils and push the rules. So, if there is evidence of academies 'off-rolling' pupils in the run-up to an Ofsted inspection or in the years where tests or GCSE examinations are to be taken, it is for the greater good. Come on, we all do it, academies or LA schools. Head teachers understand the need for good results if they are to keep their highly paid jobs and if this means 'losing' 'awkward' or less able pupils, then so be it. It is obvious that to look the best, a little of this 'redistribution' must take place but make sure it is not TOO out of line with the average. The ways are many to reduce the numbers of those who will not do credit to your academy: a few fixed-term exclusions and then a conversation with the parent suggesting Elective Home Education or a move; a part-time timetable will disrupt a family to the extent that they will take their child away. Perhaps you must resort to a permanent exclusion, but then ensure that the parent signs a *PEX Waiver* (withdrawal of permanent exclusion notice) so that the exclusion is 'not on the child's record for ever', and run it through the LA's Fair Access Panel; if there are problems with the LA and their cumbersome procedures, quoting at you the DfE *Statutory Guidance on Exclusions*, 2017 and the *Education (Pupil Registration) (England) Regulations*, 2006, Section 8, just call it a managed transfer and send the pupil's file to the nearest Alternative Provision, inform the parent and your job is done. The competition is cut-throat and money is short so no one, except the Blob, will be surprised that academies put the brakes on the numbers and types of special needs pupils they take.

Staff retention

You will be aware that current trends are leading to a crisis in recruitment and retention of teachers, and each day it is possible to see expensive media advertising aimed at attracting new recruits. These problems are said to be due to salaries not keeping up with inflation and a government refusing to fund fully the recommendations of its own pay review body. So who wants to join the teaching profession? Most teachers leaving the profession, many after just a few years, quote workload and the stress of constant target setting and aggressive monitoring of their work as being the main reasons for their disillusionment. Wimps, all of them. Why waste the investment put into training if they have not got the stamina and resilience to stick with the job? These so-called dedicated teachers say they *enjoy the teaching* and have a sense of *making an important contribution to society*, but need to *get their lives back* by working with a more reasonable work/life balance in a place where their efforts are valued and not constantly denigrated. It is all rather pathetic. In 2015, four out of every ten new teachers had left by the end of their first year in the classroom (Independent, 31 March 2015). In 2019, a survey of 8600 teachers found that 40 per cent did not see themselves working in education in 5 years' time (BBC News, 16 April 2019). Get real, young graduates! Toughen up, you mid-career waverers! Work it out, you old crumblies! The real world is a tough place and finally we are injecting some realism into the business of education.

Privatised education brought to the masses

Some claim that academisation is responsible for the supposed depressed state of the workforce – teachers and ancillary staff. Academies and free schools are not required to adhere to national terms and conditions for staff and, with the welcome decline of trade union power and influence, employees feel unsupported if they challenge any new conditions of service when joining such establishments. For existing staff, there will almost certainly be a re-structuring of posts when schools convert, that will involve signing contracts with greatly reduced rights. That is necessary to break the slovenly hold on poor practice in our schools and no apologies should be made for this.

Luckily, academies do not have to employ teachers with Qualified Teacher Status. Unqualified teachers are employed in many of these establishments and any ancillary staff are taken over by contractors imposing gig economy status on their staff. This is the way forward for an education service that is going to prove attractive to investors, yield a profit and function like a twenty-first century business operation.

It has been said that pupils are short-changed in these academies, just because the curriculum is diminished to concentrate on subjects that will boost the school's league table position and ensure the continued employment of the head teacher and senior staff. Not at all. There is no truth in this. Art subjects must be squeezed out and creativity and imagination opportunities discouraged in the endless pursuit of examination success. Right on! Practical subjects have virtually disappeared from a lot of secondary schools and this trend has been accelerated in academies and free schools for the obvious good of all. Good job too, as it is clear to *everyone* who has a brain that academic subjects are the be all and end all.

What a difference between the bright shining efficient NOW and the old-fashioned, so-called enlightened period that followed the Second World War where authorities like the world-renowned ILEA (Inner London Education Authority) built comprehensive schools where all pupils experienced practical, academic and creative subjects and then chose the areas that suited them for deeper studies at examination level. That is history and good riddance. Many of these schools had expensive, well-equipped workshops for practical lessons and were built with generous sports facilities. (see Chapter 6 on the decline in vocational subjects) Boys and girls were expected to experience in the early years of secondary education all the subjects on offer. These schools began to change the landscape of education and broke down the idea that only some pupils deserve the time, money and encouragement to succeed. This movement was greatly assisted by the abolition of most grammar schools and that 'pernicious' 11-plus exam that selected 20 per cent of the nation's 11-year-olds to 'succeed' and the vast majority of children to feel less valued and less clever. The obviously overplayed long-term psychological damage inflicted through this system has been mentioned by adults who recall their failure at this stage in their education and shamelessly exaggerate the detrimental effect it had on their sense of worth. This is a tough world with winners and losers, the deserving and the undeserving, a meritocracy we all have to get used to.

Such was the ridiculous optimism of the post-war educational scene that it became possible to think that even the private sector of education could be absorbed and organisations like CASE (Campaign for the Advancement of State Education) were formed and became influential in the education debate. The move away from these wishy-washy progressive ideas meant that CASE dropped 'Advancement' from its title and now campaigns to *defend* state education from the advances of privatisations and the narrowing of the meaning of 'education'. Fortunately, the ILEA was abolished by the Thatcher government despite a huge campaign by educationalists in Britain and abroad to retain its unique and renowned reputation for innovative, progressive and successful work in schools and Further, Adult and Early Years education.

Now there is an increased emphasis on testing right down to the very early years of schooling, even though dappy, well-meaning academics find that very young children do not develop well under the kind of pressures that have become the norm.

It is said in that liberal-leftie, *Blobby* sort of way that class teachers are best able to monitor and target the needs of individual pupils and that need and potential are not best judged or advanced by national tests that, by their very nature, are not 'child-centred'. An important sense of competiveness seeps into even the nursery and reception years, gathers pace through key stages 1 and 2 and is picked up by parents and carers who resort to private tutors to push their children up the ladder to the nearest grammar school or the preferred comprehensive even if it involves long and difficult journeys or even a house move, sometimes just temporarily, to get into the catchment area of a 'successful' school. There is also competition for a place at a 'good' private school if grammar or acceptable comprehensives are not available, an option for families with money as has ever been the case.

We should continue to build a society where competition is a by-word for progress and put a stop to any emphasis on promoting a co-operative model of human society. Education should be increasingly geared towards consumption and economic growth. We must stop worrying that the planet may not be able to maintain this growth and that it will lead to conflict and the destruction of the natural world. It is old hat to believe that education should and could help to create a different set of outcomes where we energise future adults to think outside the box and create a sustainable world that values a caring and less aggressive attitude to success and goals. However, if these values return, the academies will surely see the value of them, but only as selling points, and incorporate them into presentations of themselves on the web in that flexible, dynamic, business-like way for which they are rightly known.

A land far away

There is a secret not to be shared. There is a country with an education system that is extremely successful and bangs on proudly about the belief in investing in the value of every child and the importance of developing a cohesive society. Finland. Little Finland (population 5.5M), once land of Nokia and saunas, achieves educational outcomes that always figure at the top of international comparison tables[17]. As well as success in terms of individual achievements, it is near the top of adult 'contentment' charts despite the long winter days of darkness. The education system in Finland seems to encapsulate most of the progressive ideas that were being encouraged in Great Britain until the 80s:

1. The vital importance of play in the early years and a continuing emphasis on exploration and social interaction;
2. No formal schooling until age 7;
3. Shorter school days;
4. No homework;
5. Co-education throughout;
6. No private schools (with a few specialist exemptions);
7. No school uniform;
8. Teacher assessment up to Key Stage 4 (no national testing);
9. No league tables;
10. Two-year Teacher Training in university;
11. Teachers continuing professional development to Masters level;
12. Qualified teachers well-paid and respected as professionals;
13. Every pupil valued;
14. Children attending their local schools ensuring a sense of community and parental involvement;
15. Subjects given due weight including practical and creative areas of the curriculum;
16. And then pupils call their teachers by their first names!

Whatever next? It will never last and its self-satisfaction will go the way of Nokia. Can one really swallow the claims that their education contributes to the society being more economically equal and more at peace with itself, that young people emerge from this system as well-educated, with good mental health, open and articulate citizens who want to continue acquiring skills and knowledge into adult life? One can question the impartiality of the Organisation for Economic Co-operation and Development (OECD), which oversees so many of these measures. And you are truly lost if you can swallow such philosophising as: 'There is no word for accountability in Finnish...accountability is what is left when responsibility has been subtracted' (Pasi Sahlberg) and 'Real winners do not compete' (Samuli Paronen). Want to know who these people are? Google them!

Regardless of high taxation, generous social provision and very low levels of poverty in this quaint little country, it has no relevance at all to state schools in England, too many of which are failing young people. The privatised academy sector can rectify the ills and forge ahead to a different sort of dynamic, glittering future, from the CEOs unashamedly and deservedly on the highest salaries, through the trimmed down teaching force to the most disadvantaged learners.

3. Cut budgets to local authorities and direct the money elsewhere

Introduction

Privatisers must know their rivals and dare not wait for them to wither – crush them. Doing it slowly can be almost pleasurable. Local authorities running services with public money is almost socialism, and we know how that goes. Any service, absolutely any service, can be run better and cheaper by private operators, entrepreneurs, people with energy and creativity plus an edge of ruthlessness – because they know they are right and the profit motive works (the probation service aside).

The performance of local authorities

In 2019, there were 152 Local Authorities (LAs), a number which has increased through government legislation which sought to unify control over a number of state provided services, through the creation of unitary authorities. Much of the impact for education, marvellous in conception, comes from the Education Reform Act of 1988[18]. *Local Management of Schools* (LMS) gave greater decision-making to schools, decisions about finance, staffing, repairs etc. At this time, the 'incorporation' of FE colleges took place, making them independent of LAs. It was part of the opening of the way for schools to follow and, by 1998, 1196 schools had opted to become grant maintained. In addition, in many cases county councils were broken up to allow smaller groupings to have a role. The Inner London Education Authority, the biggest beast in the field, known worldwide as ILEA and remembered with pride and affection by many, was divided in 1990 into the 14 inner London boroughs we have today. After the Labour party came to power in 1997, LMS largely remained but it was a simple process to return those grant-maintained schools to LA control. Action by the Conservative-led coalition government from 2010, and the Conservatives alone from 2015, shows how politicians have learnt and have ensured that there will be no easy turning of academies back to LAs. This has been made very difficult with long leases on land and other legal safeguards, and anyway has already reached a proportion of the schools way beyond what the grant maintained legislation achieved over 20 years earlier. Legally locked into long-term deals, they are safe.

If rubbishing LAs has been effectively accomplished, the next step is clearly about diminishing, even extinguishing, LAs' control and influence. Firstly, by supercharging the school privatisation trend so that, instead of only failing schools being encouraged to become academies with extra funding and offers of new buildings and £2M from the sponsor (up to 2010), the offer became 'freedom' for *all* schools to apply to become academies. 'Freedom'. It's a good word. Who speaks against freedom? Once schools are no longer in the hands of local authorities the services to support schools are also freed up. Indeed, they are often willingly floated off by the local authorities to be community mutuals or employee buyouts and those employed in them are encouraged to think of this as 'an opportunity'. They are drawn into the edu-business.

It took a while to get here and we should not forget our free market history. It started with Mrs Thatcher's deceptively attractive plans to sell off council housing (forgetting why it was built in the post-war period), then continued by selling off nationalised utilities like electricity, water, telecommunications. Many of us bought into the utilities sell-off and thought ourselves very clever. As the contracting out of health, prisons and probation and other aspects of social care proceeded apace, worries have mounted, as these were seen as vital safety net and social protection services. Then came education, slowly at first, but at a national government budgetary allocation of £89 billion it was a target not to be missed by private enterprise. Blair's government, with the first city academies in 2001, inadvertently opened the door to private enterprise and nobody worried. When these enterprises fail, like the probation service now being returned to public control, it is a warning. Let us hope this does not happen to MATs. How will CEOs, who have climbed the ladder through sheer effort and skill, manage to pay off their mortgages on second and third homes [afterthought: no need to worry – generous severance and pension agreements were in place]?

If you have successfully won the hearts and minds engagement you will have shown that the people should not trust government, locally or centrally, to run education or any other service. The way is open to now hit local authorities where it hurts – in the centrally allocated funding arena.

Limitations of state control

The long-overdue criticism made by the right-wing popular press was that the national education system in England was not fit for purpose, not well directed and not well managed locally, nor even democratic. There had been a messy and unnecessary sharing of oversight of the curriculum and testing by an organisation set up as a coalition of central government, local government and the teacher unions to advise government on school examinations and curriculum changes. This was the Schools Council, which was set up in 1964 and terminated in 1984[19]. It oversaw a very wide range of innovation in the curriculum and supported 180 teacher centres around the country where teachers got together to share ideas, produce local materials and devise activities relevant to children in their areas. Thankfully all now gone, and good riddance. Local democracy is not perfect and local groups working together using local enthusiasm is not always the most professionally insightful arrangement, even if it has an old-world charm about it, and that is a waste of money.

There have long been arguments about the limitations of

central government's control of education and of variable local authorities' capacities to run their schools. ILEA is gone, all the more loved by the Blob since being swept away in 1989 and education in London is now run by 32 boroughs. Local authorities vary in size of school population from a county like Kent (250,000) or a city like Birmingham (210,000), to small ones like Hartlepool (15,000) and the smaller London boroughs such as Islington, and Kensington & Chelsea (25,000 each). Their diminished power and impoverishment is as it should be and a brilliant accomplishment of the forces of business, leaving the big decisions in the hands of our powerful friends in Parliament who run the country so well with slick decision-making (Brexit aside) and give private enterprise the chance to run the education business with reduced supervision and weakened regulation, which privatisers have been able to influence anyway. Where it goes wrong, as it surely will time and again, laugh it off with a joke (see Chapter 4 on ATT CEO Cleland's 'necessary' luxury Jaguar).

What has my local council ever done for me?

Older relations and acquaintances will reminisce about the war, the second one that is, and about how in the years that followed, thousands of council houses were built and how the council would be round to mend things that went wrong, fixing the boiler and renewing the exterior painting was always done by them. The council ran our schools, funded youth clubs and supported churches or organisations that ran them. They funded fun things like fetes, gave grants to fishing clubs, kept municipal football pitches trimmed and even paid for teams' shirts. The council was a direct employer and managed rubbish collection, road sweeping and upkeep of pavements and roads. The health service was national, but the community health services were run by councils and there were inputs to all sorts of other services. Care for the elderly and disabled still falls very much to the local councils and that is, and should be, of good quality. The trouble was that we had to pay for them – rates, taxes and levies of various sorts – and we, the public, did not like it. It cost way too much, gave too many people a comfortable, secure work life and delivered too little. That was the story to be peddled. It was not necessary to substantiate these claims with evidence; it is enough to keep on saying it. Another little trick is to point to one example of a local authority performing badly, calling it 'loony', and the dirt can spread across them all. As a form of organisation and funding of services it had had its day. All that red tape and bureaucracy could be swept away. Forms for everything, in triplicate and loads of jobs-worths gone. Wonderful. Except the forms will always be with us, just different ones.

Now, whatever money went to the councils from central government could be cut[20], and the austerity message has given this every justification. Between 2010 and 2020, the 168 councils in England will have lost 60p in every £1 previously received from government. Much of this funding is now in the hands of private sector organisations where it can be used more effectively.

Local democracy
We need to think carefully about what we want from local democracy and what services we want local politicians to run. 'Very few', is the common answer because of local councils' wastefulness, incompetence, inflexibility and inability to change. That's the story and, because it is patently true, at least never successfully countered by the local democracy lobby, the number of staff employed directly by local authorities has diminished by approximately 60 per cent in the last 10 years.

Services previously run by the council have been contracted out into a sector where, as with the academies, people at the top earn a lot, even if it is claimed without evidence that services are themselves reduced in both extent and quality. In the few instances where shortcomings have been judged chronic, a proportion of contracted out services have been brought back into local authority control. In the Academisation Regulations that is not an option for schools. There is NO RETURN to the bad old days of local authority management of schools.

The experience of sub-contracting services to the private sector nationally and locally has largely been a success. Failure in some global entrepreneurial endeavours has led to government buyouts, as with the banks, which, when revived, are returned to private hands where they are proven to be run best – apart from the global financial crash! Some large-scale services such as East Coast Rail, prisons, probation services and social care for the elderly, to name a few, have been brought back into the public sector. On a smaller scale, some local authorities have been canny enough to recall services like rubbish collection, where performance has not been good. These instances are but a slight black mark against the free market. In the current school sector, academies, individually and collectively, just need to keep claiming – whether the evidence is there or not – that they are not just doing as well as in the earlier, local democratic control regime but are surpassing anything that was previously achieved.

Many of the services were and are vital ones and the state, locally or nationally, needs to be sure they are run properly, so the privatised sector has to give credible assurance. A few of the privatised services have been natural monopolies; water is a prime example and, while power (electricity and gas) is more obviously competitive, there are claims that the 'big six' have something like a cartel going which has given them immense profits through complex tariffs to bamboozle consumers. Other services have implications both at the local and national scale, like transport; where our trains and buses go and with what frequency is something consumers and citizens might want a say in but we can satisfy that wish through customer surveys.

Of course, there is a debate about the wisdom of privatisation but on balance it has worked. Maybe there have been a few too many failures and evidence of poor regulation but good publicity works to convince the public that we are on the right track and that local authorities are not the answer to anything. In the current school sector, academies, individually and collectively, will have to show that they are not just doing as well as in the earlier local democratic control regime but are surpassing anything that was previously achieved and we must publicise that.

In relation to privatisation, whether of education or any other service, an unfair criticism has been the co-operation (collusion?) between regulators and firms (some call it working together sensibly) and too much movement of people out of regulatory positions into high paid jobs in the industry (some call it sensible recruiting and others suggest it is pay-offs for past favours). Regulators acting on behalf of government are never paid as much as private industry will pay so the temptation to move is there, and the academy sector needs to manage its relations with regulators with care. Those regulators are Ofsted, the Education and Skills Funding Agency, the Regional Schools Commissioner and, lower down the scale, the senior management of multi-academy trusts. It is easy to see how there might be charges that these arrangements are both conveniently underpowered and insufficiently independent (see later for snuffing out complaints). While the responsibility for the Grenfell Tower fire disaster is still being unpicked, we might look at the quite different scandal of Boeing signing off its 737 Max airliner and its lack of responsiveness to reports of flaws and see that horrific disasters can follow from inadequate regulation. We must self-regulate, fairly transparently and evidence our performance in academies across the country to the enquiring public.

Schools are a big, important public service, not as big as the NHS but still big and maybe even more important than the

NHS. At any one time in England, there are 8,000,000 children in schools. There has to be a lot of business to be grabbed there by lively entrepreneurs. There should indeed be some care about who makes decisions about what this service/business provides and achieves and about how it is best regulated and the private academy sector has all that in hand.

Edu-business comes to town

Business is booming. The money is big, really big, and the tracks are laid down for good earnings to be made by enterprises that have goods and services to sell to schools. Solicitors were on hand when schools decided to become academies from 2010 and at that time there was a £25,000 grant, most of which was paid to the lawyers, some of whom were 'recruited' to governing bodies prior to conversion – just to help the process along: accountants, staff developers, human resource experts, payroll experts, recruitment 'solutions', maintenance and repairs are all on hand to help for a fee. Best of all, to display the wonderful array of services able to take a share of a school's budget now it has freedom, are the Academies and Schools Shows (watchwords for 2019: 'Learning, Collaborating, Inspiring'), which held 2-day events in London's Excel Centre and the NEC, Birmingham in 2019. 'Solutions' was a word associated with many presenters amongst the 150+ stands.

Surveyors to education, S2e, whose immediate question is 'Unsuccessful with your CIF bid?' That is a *Condition Improvement Fund* where the government has set aside £500M. They will survey, write the bid and organise the building/repairs etc as well as carrying out 'space utilisation and capacity planning'.

Portakabin, for new teaching space, and 'when you're up against the clock it helps to work with a supplier who consistently meets deadlines'. *Benchmark* will do your foldaway tables and seating.

Education solutions, recruitment solutions, truancy solutions, supply cover solutions, catering solutions are all here. How could one not want *Building Schools for Nothing* (BSfN) which 'provides consultancy services to develop unique strategies for generating funding to deliver new school buildings and facilities'? Schools often have surplus land that is not fully utilised. BSfN works to sell off these valuable land assets to generate funding to finance building projects. It is an attractive idea to sell off part of the playing fields to build a suite of classrooms.

The banks are there to look after your money, *Capita* or *Civica* for software, *Chubb* for security, *Renewable Solutions* for 'LED lighting projects (no capital outlay)', *Cornerstones* will provide cross-curricular projects for the primary school.

Some possibilities for spending your budget are truly wonderful, even futuristic:

Impero are 'enthusiasts with a passion for education and student wellbeing. 100 per cent focussed on the EdTech space, we develop cloud-based solutions in direct response to the latest education trends and requirements.'

Mindfulness in Schools Project (MiSP) aims to improve the lives of children by making a genuine, positive difference to their mental health and wellbeing.

MTM:

provide UNIQUE market insights, enabling you to realise your vision for the future. Feasibility studies, supply and demand analyses, and stakeholder research are all designed to help you understand the potential of your market, where you stand against your competitors and what the market wants. MTM will tell you where to find the RIGHT learners, HOW to reach them and WHAT'S important to them.

If you have not grasped it, MTM promises to get you a high quality, middle-class pupil intake.

Promethean 'with more than 20 years of experience in K-12 classrooms, is a global leader in education technology [whose] combined hardware and software solutions are designed to transform learning spaces into collaborative and connected environments, promote student participation and engagement throughout the learning process'.

Renaissance Learning UK Ltd is 'a leading provider of cloud-based assessments for primary and secondary schools. Our computer-adaptive Star Assessments for reading, maths and early learning can be administered to an entire class in just 20 minutes.'

Weduc will 'enable effortless teacher-parent communication via e-mail, SMS, private social media and mobile apps', encourages targeted communication and makes seamless parental engagement possible in any educational establishment.

Lecture and discussion sessions at the 2019 Academies and Schools Show also dealt with staff development, transforming governance and even 'how to generate income'.

This is a different world from the fuddy-duddy local authority school service that sauntered along in its easy-going, child-friendly way with no thought to the hard, fast world we live and work in. Indeed, EES, once Essex Education Support, has floated off to offer its services across the country, as has North Yorkshire Education Services – 'proud to announce its support for the recently launched Institute of Ethical Artificial Intelligence in Education (IEAIED)'. These agencies, once dedicated to a local area, are now *free* to pursue Edu-business wherever it is to be found. MAT chief executives and head teachers, 'free' from LA shackles, wander round goggle-eyed at all that is on offer and the invitations to lunch and 'further conversations' from pro-active sales folk are bound to follow, with the feeling that this is the superfast modern way to 'learn, collaborate and inspire', with the tax payers money obviously in the background to fund purchases.

This is the future

Local authorities could not do the job, local democracy was too cumbersome to direct schools, local education officers and advisors were too lackadaisical to develop an education fit for the twenty-first century. Schools have 'voted' to leave LA control in droves and three-quarters of secondary schools now enjoy the freedom to be creative with the curriculum, employment regulations and commissioning services and, whether in stand-alone academies or MATs, the earnings can be high.

Long gone are the days when the LA did HR, accounts, repairs, staff development, governor training and support. Edu-preneurs are here to stay and grow. No one will claim that the new school set up with private suppliers to academy chain charities wastes money and that the services a local authority once offered were economic and effective. That is a myth that is continually debunked. Moreover, some still do not accept that talent costs money and you have to pay high salaries to recruit good people. Deaf to these judgements, educational professions can feel the wow factor through all the wonderful mottos of the academies; you can string a motto together from any three or four words pulled from the motto tub. In this new era, there is the thrusting sales pitch of suppliers, with their 'passion' and straplines. Parents will be in awe. Just look at the website of a local, 'bog standard' primary school with boring old stuff on it, black print on a grey picture background so you cannot read it. OK, they say their job is teaching children, relating to parents, organising jumble sales but how about a bit of pizazz on the worldwide web.

Across the sector, new organisations have been formed to replace what LAs did. Six Regional Schools Commissioners oversee from afar more schools than all 162 local authorities. That's efficiency. They are supported by Headteacher Boards, mostly appointees. Slick stuff. Above and around them are those national communication forums which spread the government message and for which attendees pay as much as £390 for a day of wisdom. Nothing comes cheap, except the Schools and Academies Show overseen by *Govnet* which was free. *Inside Government*, a division within Govnet Communications, is a trading name of Partnership Media Group Ltd and, like *Government Events*, has an inside track on policy developments, has first-rate connections with politicians and puts on expensive one-day conferences. *Westminster Forum Projects* sets up expensive conferences in 16 policy areas and gets top speakers, no question. This is the way to manage information and local authorities are nowhere to be seen, nor are the unions nor any sense of local inputs. This is super-efficient even if some squeal that it is super-nasty.

Freedom

It is hard to believe the range of controls from which schools are freed once they are out of local authority control. It is as well to highlight them and also to be aware of the lack of enforcement. All schools have to participate in admissions arrangements, but academies can set some of their own rules. They should count themselves as part of local Fair Access Panel (FAP) arrangements, mostly for the placement of difficult children, but co-operation there can be limited. MATs can pay what they like and wriggle out of national pay scale agreements, particularly at the top end. They can off-roll brazenly and take no notice of what the LA tells them if it does not follow the DfE 2017 Guidance on Exclusions. Even in terms of national 'requirements', MATs and academies can act with breath-taking independence, defiance or just plain silence in the face of requests for information or complaints. From the top to the bottom they can get away with doing things their way and in their own time.

The Department for Education has been getting into trouble over its accounts. The 2015/16 accounts were 'qualified' over the lack of clarity in the sections incorporating academies. In subsequent years, the academy sector annual report and accounts were submitted separately but have been 14 months late, largely over issues with accounting for land and buildings which led the Comptroller and Auditor General (C&AG) to qualify his audit opinion i.e. express a concern which should be addressed. And still the committee wanted to see more information on academy performance. For example, they said there was not 'sufficiently granular analysis to enable a reader to understand the performance of the sector in detail [nor] contain benchmarks to allow parents and local communities to understand whether or not the performance of an academy trust is improving'[21]. On top of that, 88 trusts missed deadlines in submitting their accounts in 2017/18 (ESFA Report 2018), but the Agency is 'taking a firmer stance on non-compliance'. The Public Accounts Committee report in January 2019 on Academy Accounts and Performance[22] was critical of the oversight of the academy sector and, in a report 2 years before, the committee had called the new free schools funding system 'incoherent'. Lord Agnew, Parliamentary Under-Secretary of State for the School System, wrote a follow-up letter to 22 schools asking them to account for 'excessive high pay' (February 2019). The request in itself seemed a bit of a joke, especially as some of the big payers were not listed; presumably they had responded to the first letter and given a credible answer. No strident demands, no real naming and shaming and no sanctions, thus allowing them the freedom to continue as before.

4. Broadcast data about state schools failing

Looking back on a more kindly age

England in 2019 has an inspection system increasingly seen by some as operating with the prime task of identifying failure rather than promoting improvement. That may be unfortunate, but you have to weed out all that below-average practice and attainment. Everyone should be above average. The removal of 'Satisfactory' in Ofsted reporting was a ramping up of the pressure, the drive for ever greater effort and achievement. Who wants to be 'Satisfactory', and doesn't it really mean what we now call it, 'Requires Improvement'?

There is the once-upon-a-time world where teachers turned up for work moderately prepared, but equally happy to follow pupils' enthusiasms if that was what was arising. We can read of Laurie Lee's schooldays in *Cider with Rosie*, Michael Armstrong's *Closely Observed Children* or Phillida Salmon's *Coming to Know*, where she memorably gives thanks to Lesley Smith, 'who ran one of the most-hearted secondary schools in London' and later set up something called The Goldsmith's Curriculum Laboratory at that despicable and much misguidedly cherished one-time centre of progressive education, home to arch-child-centred advocates Louis Cohen and Lawrence Manion.

The authors which trainee teachers were expected to read were child-centred with the justification that 'leading out' must be taken seriously as we strive to take children from where they are to...well somewhere forward, depending to some degree on their wishes and temperament. Think of the list that current new teachers will not encounter – Ball, Bernstein, Bruner, Dewey, Lawton, Piaget, Stenhouse, White, Whitty, Vygotsky. What a waste of time that was. Who remembers what they had to say now?

Looking back at what seemed easier and pleasanter times will do little good. In those times, there were not the technologies for testing and comparing, even as recently as the 1980s. There were also not the globalised comparisons from OECD we have today from PISA, TIMSS and PIRLS[23] and Innocenti Report Cards from Unicef on *Fairness for Children: a League Table of Inequality in Child Well-being in Rich Countries*[24] also give measures where the nation can be proud, a little dissatisfied or downright dismayed. It is a veritable industry, holding a mirror up to our country's performance in education.

International comparisons show we are doing poorly

We are lucky to have these highly respectable measures making comparisons country by country on reading writing and maths. It is good to know where you stand in the world, and of course we want to be near the top, where we thought we once were. Most recently (2016), by these measures, the UK was twenty-sixth in mathematics; this was behind all those far east countries and Switzerland (eighth), Estonia (ninth) and also Netherlands, Finland and Germany and Poland and even Australia and New Zealand[25]. Since any readers would want to know, the UK was twenty-second in reading, and fifteenth equal in science, just behind little Slovenia. Rankings were slightly better in 2010: eleventh in maths, twentieth in reading and eleventh in science – embarrassing mediocrity and a slight slip down the ranking. The solution is obvious: hand over schools to the guys and girls who can 'make England great again', even if it had not quite worked up to 2015. Another report from OECD on 23 key measures on children puts the UK in the bottom third for young people's life satisfaction, including the *Not in Education, Employment or Training* (NEET) measure and adolescent fertility. Young people in Mexico and the United States report distinctly higher life satisfaction[26]. We can only conclude that schooling in England at this current time succeeds in neither high academic achievement nor in making young people happy.

Schools are lagging behind

It is common knowledge that schools, like health services, are under-funded and teacher recruitment is difficult but if we want a sympathetic government to help us to draw more schools out of the deadening grip of the local authority, then we should not make too much fuss. Though there are those 'awards' and stories of great state schools, the reports of crap schools are more striking and more frequent. Do a web search for 'England's best schools' and you get Eton, Harrow etc with their annual fees of £36,000 and upwards. Search bad schools and we get something different.

In 2017, 365 secondary schools out of the total of 3297 failed to meet the government's minimum standard of pupil progress across eight subjects – with particular weight given to English and maths in the Attainment 8 benchmark in GCSEs at 16+. That is 11.6 per cent of schools and over a quarter of a million students. *The Sun* and the *Daily Mail* run such stories annually for our edification and shame[27]. A 'full list of England's worst primary schools has finally been revealed,' says *The Sun*, 364 of them in 2018. 'BAD EDUCATION' is the *Mail's* headline. Primary schools are considered to be under-performing if less than 65 per cent of pupils reach the expected standard in reading, writing and maths at age 11. A total of 90,000 pupils are being taught in these poor schools[28].

Not all is doom and gloom as public (ie. fee-paying) schools are good, grammar schools are good, but the rest need freedom from local authorities to improve, unshackled alliances to help them do better and the leadership to drive standards up. Bad press helps to keep the door open to promote the academisation trend. Testing, testing, testing from the Early Years Foundation Stage profile (EYFS) at age 4 and 5 through Key Stage 1 (age 7), Key Stage 2 (age 11) to Key Stage 4 at 16 are tremendous weapons to beat teachers with and promote release from LAs. Inspecting and re-inspecting also disciplines schools and makes teachers answerable for results and if the attainment data can be fudged then why not (academies seem to get unfairly caught out at this).

An Ofsted inspection usually lasts 2 days and is carried out by a team of as many as five inspectors. They grade a school as outstanding, good, requires improvement (once 'satisfactory') or inadequate for overall effectiveness and then use four subcategories.

- leadership and management
- quality of teaching, learning and assessment
- personal development, behaviour and welfare
- outcomes for pupils

As of 2016, 82 per cent of the 163 grammar schools in England were judged 'outstanding' while 19 per cent of the 3000 non-selective secondary schools were given this grade. Non-selective means comprehensive and all those in selective areas that were not grammar schools[29]. Pupil numbers have been increased at grammar schools in recent years, obviously, because they are able to get those results at 16. Only 2.6 per cent of children at grammar schools are eligible for free school meals (FSM) compared with 18 per cent in other schools where the grammars are located, and more than 10 per cent of entrants to grammar schools at 11 come out of private education[30]. Maybe there is a link. It is good to see 142 out of 163, 87 per cent of grammar schools, have seen sense and converted to academies.

There were the trailblazers on comprehensivisation in the 1960s, who saw the new combined schools as 'providing a grammar school education for everyone' – full of uniform wearing, satchel carrying, homework-doing pupils. It didn't work out quite like that and we have a shoddier system getting shoddier. Solution: get private enterprise into schools to get things working.

Local authority schools are doing really *badly*

While the country's schools are at best mediocre at the core business, they are poor at all that citizenship, social emotional wellbeing and general behaviour development – except the grammars and the public schools, of course. Knife crime, truancy, out-of-control youngsters and what are the schools doing about these social ills? They complain about lack of funding, the youth service wiped out, careers guidance a joke, teaching assistant posts slashed, family link workers largely a memory and even young offender institutions unable to cope. Are these really the causes of today's social problems? There are complaints about the state of school buildings and staff having to do cleaning and maintenance. Teachers are said to be over-worked and apparently staff absenteeism is on the increase. The private sector knows about working efficiently, managing staff effectively and making savings wisely and can be safely left to sort this out – as they are doing.

It is in the interests of academy leaders, as edu-preneurs, to at least maintain the claim that there was a large block of lumpen, 'bog standard' and certainly unimpressive schools that needed saving. The issue of Academy Orders to require schools to become academies if judged 'inadequate' by Ofsted confirms the privatised sector as the saviours. The story is persuasive and winning. The razzamatazz and the ability to blunt most criticism, and in some cases having the nerve to just laugh it off, is much to academy leaders' credit. This extends from the news on chief executive Ian Cleland's XJ Premium Luxury V6 Jaguar (ATT – 'Transparency, Innovation, Collaboration, Ambition') to the CEO of the Paradigm Trust ('Integrity, Excellence, Community') on £195,000, with added perks. Then there is Steve Kenning of Aspirations Academies Trust ('Transforming Learning in the Digital Age') earning a cool £225,000, whose wife as executive principal and co-founder is on a slightly less cool £175,000. Academies as a whole are in the leading spot in the '*Do you believe your school has ever excluded a pupil or encouraged them to leave in order to improve the school's results?'* stakes: 18 per cent sponsored academies; 14 per cent converter academies; the rest (meaning LA schools) come in at about 10 per cent. None of this is related in reports to <u>achievement</u>, the sector's number one concern.

Just keep saying that academies are the best, brazen out the big bucks pay deals, ease out children who are obviously not right for you and your establishment and carry on with the necessary staff culling.

Ancillary services for children are doing especially badly if you can find them at all

Wider services for children and families are appalling, if they are there at all. And who needs them? Sure Start has all but disappeared, family outreach units are gone, social services have more children to deal with than they can manage, Child and Adolescent Mental Health Services have always had long waiting lists with thresholds raised higher and the youth service has all but disappeared. Numbers of cases referred have risen by 26 per cent over the 5 years to 2017, nearly a quarter are rejected and others have long waits[31], but all this is for others outside education to solve. With austerity, more children are in poverty but whose fault is that? We are all individuals and decision-makers for ourselves and our families, and some people and families and their children make bad decisions. It is no concern of the academised school sector to bail them out.

A class curriculum

Schools are places where children are sent to learn in a disciplined environment; it is as simple as that. If all organisations just kept their eye on the ball (so to speak) and got on with the core business the world would be a better place. In schools, we have a curriculum to deliver, that's right, *deliver*. Know the subject, organise your delivery and set to.

Having freedom from local authority control means deciding for ourselves what the content and organisation of the curriculum should be and enables us to rid ourselves of the soft options, the BTEC courses, community care and media studies. This class curriculum is high class, concentrating on the basics (because those are the things that are measured) putting pressure on the students to perform and concentrating on genuine academic subjects.

Discipline, discipline, discipline

If the curriculum is going to work, then as well as a team of teachers who know their subject matter, at primary or secondary level, you need DISCIPLINE and that extends from full uniform, through insistence that all homework is done, having all necessary materials with you for lessons, to complete acquiescence in the classroom. The young people will have time to participate and argue with adults when they are grown up but if our performance and results are to match our mottos and our hype, we must hold firm on the discipline front. Certainly, academies can outstrip the local authority schools in the behaviour and uniform stakes.

To help the staff body in delivering the agreed, simple curriculum, we need a discipline policy and if it extends to zero tolerance, that is fine. Whatever works, and do not allow child psychology to be quoted to you. The kids are just the learners and you want them to soak up the learning. Discipline policies in schools should be comprehensive and cover ALL eventualities. Ark John Keats Academy has a model policy the like of which you will (surely) find in no local authority school. It is right that there should be lots of rules for behaviour in the classrooms where the learning is to take place. The decision to regulate behaviour in every part of the school day in this discipline policy is monstrously impressive and certainly necessary.

At 8:25am a member of staff will raise their arm. All pupils will immediately raise their arm and wait in silence for further instruction, to line up in tutor or class groups. A uniform and equipment check will take place at this time or at the start of lesson 1. Staff will check their line and ensure there is 100 per cent compliance with the routines – STAR position, both straps of bag on shoulders, looking directly ahead and wearing the correct uniform.

Courtyard rules mention 'normal conversation, groups of less than 6,' *so there are two things they had better get right.*

During break and lunchtime all pupils will:

a. At break be walked to the external door of the block in STAR lines, before being dismissed to break by their teacher.

b. For wet breaks be instructed to go to designated areas.

c. At lunch to be walked in STAR lines either to the dining hall, or to the courtyard.

d. Sit at their tutor group or enrichment table, in allocated seats to ensure a family dining type of atmosphere.

e. Go, speaking in paired conversation tone, for food when directed by the tutor or teacher. School meals are compulsory for all pupils at the academy at KS3. KS4 pupils will be able to opt for a packed lunch on a term-by-term basis. Parental consent will be required.

f. Thank catering staff as they are served.

g. Engage in polite table talk/discuss the thought for the day with classmates.

h. Take turns to have responsibility for cleaning up as part of their tutor group service, which will be directed by the tutor. Pupils leave the table silently as a group and are escorted to the relevant outside area by their tutor.

i. Meet friends to talk in the internal courtyard areas. Group sizes are to be a maximum of 6. A warning, and checks will be given if numbers exceed this.

j. Bring permitted healthy food and snacks to be eaten at

break time.

k. Walk calmly and use the paired conversation tone in the courtyards. Checks will be given immediately for infringements of this.

l. Read or revise in the library, or take part in an indoor extra-curricular activity. Ensure that a calm and purposeful atmosphere is maintained in these areas.

m. Meet with staff to address any concerns or queries. Staff on duty will circulate during break and lunchtime.

n. The Head of Year (HoY) or another member of staff will raise an arm at the end of break and lunch. All pupils must immediately raise their arms in silence, track the member of staff and await instruction. Once instruction has been given by HoY, pupils should walk in silence directly to tutor/lesson/enrichment line.

o. Attend lunchtime Catch Ups. It is the pupil's responsibility to attend any lunchtime catch-up (see sanctions policy).

At the end of the academy day, all pupils will say the pledge, led by their teacher or tutor, before being dismissed. (There is more to be learnt from North Korea and the USA.)

The *a* to *o* of behavioural instructions is phenomenal in the detail and, as for the pledge, it was bound to be something near religious, to make you feel guilty if you don't comply, like 'Being the best that I can be' or 'Being polite and helpful to everyone in the whole world every minute of the day'. It never hurts to have the highest aspirations, even when utterly unattainable, but the Ark John Keats Academy pledge is actually:

I believe that I can always learn and improve.

I am committed to working hard so I will realise my full potential.

I treat others with respect at all times.

I know that KINDNESS, EFFORT, ASPIRATION and

TENACITY bring SUCCESS.

Get out your most extravagant 'Founding vision and values' like 'To ensure that every pupil succeeds, regardless of socio-economic background, by providing outstanding teaching and pastoral care' and 'To become the best school in London by 2020' (Ark Greenwich Free School). Do not hold back. Give yourself the best press you can.

Evidence showing how great academies are
Let us look at:

1. Achievement
2. Financial management
3. Inspection
4. Turning schools around
5. Governance

To have a set of schools out of local democratic control and show that they perform better than the poor, neglected ones back where they were in the 50s, 60s etc is the goal. Having rubbished the rest, we look for the data that shows academies are best.

1. Achievement
As of June 2018, here it is. The Education Policy Institute[32] writes that:

'Overall, we find little difference in the performance of schools in academy chains and local authorities. The type of school – academy or local authority – is therefore less important than being in a *high-performing school group*.

We find that both academy chains and local authorities feature at the very top of our performance tables, and at the very bottom.

Primary school performance_

Examining the impact that both school types have on pupil improvement, and accounting for pupil characteristics, we find:

Local authorities make up 15 of the top 20 school groups at Key Stage 2. This is slightly higher than would be expected, taking into account the total number of LAs and academy chains.

The highest performing academy chain is the Harris Federation, the only academy chain amongst the top 10.

Academy chains are over-represented in the lowest performing groups. In the bottom 20 of all school groups, 11 are academy chains.

The lowest performing academy chains include Wakefield City Academies Trust and the Education Fellowship Trust, both of which have subsequently relinquished all of their schools.

Secondary school performance

Academy chains feature heavily in the top 20 performing school groups: 14 of the top 20 are academy chains.

The highest performing academy chain is the Rodillian Academy. The highest performing large trusts are Outwood Grange and the Harris Federation.

The highest performing local authorities include Brent, Hackney and Kingston-upon-Hull. Of the six local authorities that are in the top 20, five are in London.

The lowest performing academy chains at Key Stage 4 include the Bright Tribe Trust, the Hart Schools Trust and the Education Fellowship Trust. The Bright Tribe Trust has relinquished all but one of its schools in the north of England while keeping its schools in the south.

The lowest performing local authorities include Nottingham, Southend-on-Sea and Barnsley. Subsequently, more schools in Nottingham have become academies.

Policy implications: When we compare these latest results with those from our report on performance in 2015, we find

cases of sustained underperformance in both academy chains and local authorities.

A Department for Education report[33] for January 2017 headlines:

'At key stage 2, more than half the MATs had above average progress in writing and maths. However, on the measure of reading progress over half of the MATs have scores that are below average, and at key stage 4, two-thirds of the MATs had progress 8 scores that were below average.'

Aaah, that was not as convincing as had been hoped, but do not despair.

2. Financial management

On the money side of things academies should come out better. The House of Commons Committee of Public Accounts in its academy accounts and performance (January 2019)[34] begins with a paragraph which goes:

There has been a succession of high-profile academy failures that have been costly to the taxpayer [damn] and damaging to children's education [blast]. Some academy trusts have misused public money through related-party transactions and paying excessive salaries. At Durand Academy Trust and Bright Tribe Trust, there were serious failures of governance and oversight. This cannot be allowed to happen again – governance at academy trusts needs to be stronger and the Department for Education's oversight and intervention needs to be more rigorous. The Education and Skills Funding Agency (ESFA) is taking steps to control executive pay and related-party transactions, but these actions are as yet unproven and in isolation will not prevent abuse. We expect to return to these issues in future.

That hurts a little but it can be disregarded. Academies and

MATs should make sure it does not go to extremes and that there are not too many examples of misuse of funds, related-party transactions and super-bumper salaries...which should be hidden, or wrapped up in bonuses which do not show on the annual accounts.

3. Inspections

At inspections, academies should be good, indeed very good

A Local Government Association Report[35] taking inspections up to December 2017 shows graphically that of the 14,000 LA schools inspected, 91 per cent were Outstanding or Good. Of the 6000 academies inspected, the comparable rate was 86 per cent.

Damn it all, that is not showing academies up in a good light, well, not as good as friends in government would expect after all the money they have thrown at the sector.

4. Turning schools around

This is something at which academies should excel. The claim is that academies have resources and know-how to do far better than the weak and cumbersome LAs in supporting school improvement.

An LGA report[36] was taken up by a journalist under the headline, **Councils better at turning around failing schools than academy chains**, which was not what the academy sector was comfortable with. It gave details:

The report looked at 429 council-run schools rated as inadequate in 2013, found that 115 **(75 per cent)** of 152 schools that stayed with the council became good or outstanding by 2017, but that only 92 **(59 per cent)** of the 155 schools that had been inspected since becoming sponsored academies saw their Ofsted ratings improve to good or outstanding.

An unwanted comment and ill-informed judgement on

academies' and MATS' capacity to improve, said, 'It is not fair on children and parents to be denied the chance of a better education because their local council is barred from helping.'

Luckily, Lord Agnew, the Academies Minister, rebutted the conclusions with pithy statements. While not the sharpest statistician or even arithmetician in the drawer, Agnew said that:

The LGA's interpretation of this analysis is deeply flawed. The data actually underlines why our reforms were necessary and morally right, by pointing out how many under-performing schools were taken out of local authority control and turned into academies...unsurprising that local authorities fare better in an analysis which excludes schools that had failed under their leadership. It does not say anything about the effectiveness of sponsored academies.

While this may look quite damning, with smoke, rebuttal and counter-claim, developments can continue as before. No one retains the detail for long.

5. Governance

Academies, as limited companies, choose their own governing bodies. The individual academy has no legal entity apart from the MAT of which it is part. There is no requirement to have parent or staff representation and certainly no local authority input. Academies over all are collectively represented by the **Confederation of School Trusts**, which has board members with impressive credentials. There are CEOs of trusts, award-winning head teachers, ex-directors of education in local authorities and a CBE. Also in evidence is the Academy Ambassadors service which aims at 'building better trust boards', 'recruiting the right people with the right skills', the first three skills of which in the list are 'Auditing', 'branding and marketing' and 'CEO and general management'. Obviously, no educational background is needed and no local knowledge, commitment or sensitivity. By emphasising the business skills of trust boards both local knowledge and educational knowledge are rightly devalued. The picture on the front of the flyer offering to find governors or trustees is of four smart business people; of course it includes one female and one ethnic minority, but still looks corporate and not at all smiling or local. Presenting the Academy Ambassadors in this way could seem like an own goal and not very clever. On the other hand, if we are talking big business, then perhaps they have got it right.

Never mind the data if it does not fit

On top of that gleeful cry from the democratic and local accountability Blob crowd over the absurd 'no discernable difference' or 'councils do it better' or 'they can't handle the money' conclusions, the academy sector, the bright, shining, new, innovative, just-do-it academy sector, is accused of *gaming* the system to artificially accumulate the best results. Gaming? Of course! Off-rolling students? Well, yes, because academies cannot go through all the local authority Fair Access Panel rigmarole. Why should an independent academy listen to the local authority officers at all? Academies do not have a legal responsibility to educate *all* children and it is known which children will do well, and they are the ones for the academies.

Anyway, all this data is out of date, the criticisms are of a few bad apples and academies get the job done, do not moan (too much) about cuts and austerity, understand it is necessary and trim budgets accordingly. The conclusion we want people left with is that England's schools are failing, that local authorities have shown they are not up to system improvement and the academy revolution can save them.

5. Sing the praises of Standards not Structures

Mindblowing

It is nothing short of mindblowingly obvious that these terms should mark the polarisation in educational debate. Some have argued that it is mindblowingly awful and ask in their namby-pamby way, 'Where are children in all this?' The answer is that the children/pupils/students are the raw material we are working on with which (whom?) we need to reach high standards of academic attainment. We, the privatisers and entrepreneurs, know that you get high standards by narrowing the curriculum, assessing, grading and testing, eliminating children you don't want when you can and fiddling the figures if no one is watching. Structures don't matter provided the working within them is effective.

Education is a public service for ALL young people and the freedom exists for those with money to buy something better still – a set of arguments for another time. In this world of *individuals*, there are some who have outstanding talent and there are others who are not much good at anything. Some will argue that state education provision is not about standards or structures but about children, their communities, inclusion to the extent that they remain in education feeling good about it for as long as it has something to offer them, and a system might be judged by how well it does by its most needy and most challenging. Another argument for another time!

It is mindblowing to think we can educate all children in the same institutions. We have our special schools for those with particular levels of diagnosed needs. Why not specially designed schools for the brightest and those who are recognised as the ones who will go far, often from an early age?

Grammar Schools

Grammar schools are for the brightest and the best and the pity is that we have only 163 in the country, though numbers of pupils within them are thankfully growing with the recognition that this is what parents want. There are only nine schools in Scotland called grammar, but the title is really only a recognition of a long and prestigious history, and in reality they are treated like any other high school. There are none of these excellent schools in Wales, yet 67 in Northern Ireland, where over 40 per cent of students attend these selective schools; when it is getting on for half the cohort it makes a nonsense of 'selection'. Lefties claim that selective education is ineffective, a morally dubious preserve of social elites, a middle-class affair. So what? Results are an indication of worth. You only have to look at attainment and the judgements of inspections.

GCSE results, shown in a government report, give achievement in 2015 of mainstream secondary schools for 5A*–C including English and maths as 57 per cent for comprehensives (500,000 pupils), 97 per cent for grammars (22,000 pupils) and 50 per cent for secondary moderns (20,000 pupils)[37]. Added to that, 80 per cent of grammars are awarded an Ofsted grade of 'outstanding' against just 18 per cent for the rest.

Poverty, attainment and failure

The argument is made that a school or academy stands a better chance of an 'outstanding' or 'good' Ofsted grade the fewer free school meals pupils it has. The bar graph below omits ethnic minorities (not sure why) but covers all 3158 secondary schools with the relevant data available. Just look at that: very low levels of deprivation (top bar) and over half will be judged 'outstanding', the type of place any middle-class parent would want their child to attend. Nearly half of the schools with 29 per cent+ FSM pupils, the highest 'deprivation' category, are 'requires improvement' or 'inadequate' (33 + 14).

Overall effectiveness grades of secondary schools by proportion of pupils who are White British and eligible for free school meals (Ofsted, 2018)

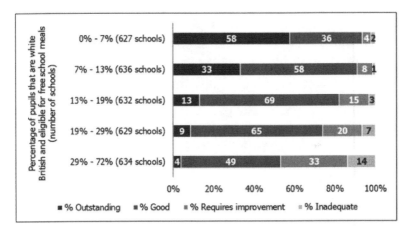

All schools should be good or better and we have to thrash the below-average schools to get them to pull themselves together and start teaching well. It is not the *type* of school (er, independents and grammars have a bit of an advantage), it is teaching quality and, despite what the statistics show, how long can we go on blaming poverty? If poverty were accepted as a CAUSE of low attainment in schools and poor performance of schools, then the state would have done something to alleviate poverty. Wouldn't it?

School governing bodies spend an inordinate amount of meeting time considering the minutia of test and exam predictions and results, and these discussions dominate the agenda. These considerations can only happen as a result of hours of collation by subject leaders and classroom teachers who are increasingly pressured to spend time and effort on what they think is of little advantage to the pupils. There is in the staffroom, where staffrooms still exist, (another good 'divide and rule' tactic – the last thing you want is teachers sharing complaints and generally griping), a saying imported from the farm, that, 'You don't fatten the pig by constantly weighing it,' a backward-looking and inappropriate adage. This analysis must go on, whether in local authority schools or academies, primary just as much as secondary. A key purpose is to keep the focus on the schools as the solution to inequalities related to income and class, which of course they can never be. We will just pretend so that we do not get drawn into the bigger, insoluble issues about responsiveness to social need, and responsibility for both diversity and social justice.

Education for all

Education has never been very good at compensating for social ills, most notably poverty. We keep urging that schools should and can overcome difficulties associated with poor home background, which is why we have the Pupil Premium Grant, the extra money for pupils who have been on free school meals at any time in the previous 6 years, looked after children and forces children. School governors are largely oblivious to how this flawed, if well-meaning, policy fails, as evidence is showing the strategy will not overcome drawbacks that accompany child poverty. Heaven help the head teacher who suggests that low measured attainment in his or her school is something to do with families on low incomes and the associated culture. All in the teaching profession know that you can improve your results by improving your intake, but it cuts no ice with politicians, national or local. Just knowing the spread of attainment and how, year after year, it <u>does</u> relate to socio-economic status, things like being on benefits or earning so little the child is on free school meals, and try as you might, you cannot get the results. Add to that the statistics on exclusion, fixed period and permanent, and we get the same message. Deep down we know it is not about making a few families more affluent but raising the basic levels of income, improving housing and diet and making available generally more uplifting and developmental opportunities for young people.

Income Deprivation Affecting Children Index (IDACI) deciles and percentages reaching 'expected levels' of attainment in England in 2015 (2012 figures in brackets)

IDACI DECILE	KS 1 Level 2 reading, writing & maths % (age 7)	KS 2 Level 4 reading, writing & maths % (age 11)	KS 4 ~ 5A*-C GCSEs including Eng & maths % (age 16)
Poorest 10%	73.4 (66.7)	63.3 (57.0)	39.2 (34.9)
11 - 20%	76.3 (71.1)	65.0 (59.7)	40.9 (37.6)
21 - 30%	79.3 (74.6)	68.0 (63.9)	44.7 (42.0)
31 - 40%	81.3 (77.4)	70.6 (66.9)	48.6 (45.5)
41 - 50%	83.7 (80.2)	73.9 (70.0)	53.0 (50.2)
51 - 60%	85.8 (82.5)	76.6 (74.0)	57.7 (55.3)
61 - 70%	87.2 (84.7)	79.0 (76.5)	61.6 (59.7)
71 - 80%	88.6 (86.1)	81.2 (78.8)	65.4 (63.6)
81 - 90%	89.8 (87.9)	83.5 (81.3)	68.8 (67.4)
Most affluent 10%	91.6 (90.1)	86.4 (84.6)	74.6 (73.0)
FREE SCHOOL MEALS			
FSM	72.1 (64.5)	59.2 (53.0)	32.8 (29.4)
Non-FSM	87.5 (84.5)	79.9 (76.2)	63.8 (59.0)
GENDER			
Girls	87.4 (84.2)	76.9 (71.8)	64.1 (61.5)
Boys	79.3 (75.0)	71.3 (69.2)	54.2 (50.7)

Total numbers: around 500,000. Source: National Pupil Database analyses of two longitudinal cohorts

It should not go unnoticed that girls' measured performance at every key stage is higher than that of boys. Exclusion rates for girls are about one-fifth those of boys.

Permanent and fixed period exclusions by level of deprivation of school in England 2016/17 (2014/15 figures in brackets)

	Number of schools	Permanent exclusions		Fixed period exclusions	
		Number	%	Number	%
Poorest 10%	1991	980	**0.13** (0.11)	50,590	**6.48** (5.36)
10-20%	2044	990	**0.12** (0.08)	47,990	**5.72** (4.60)
20-30%	2028	990	**0.12** (0.09)	44,675	**5.32** (4.34)
30-40%	1982	885	**0.11** (0.09)	39,885	**4.89** (4.49)
40-50%	2076	785	**0.09** (0.08)	41,805	**5.01** (4.23)
50-60%	2216	745	**0.09** (0.07)	39,040	**4.78** (3.74)
60-70%	2246	610	**0.08** (0.05)	31,660	**4.11** (3.34)
70-80%	2325	700	**0.09** (0.06)	32,670	**4.23** (2.99)
80-90%	2346	605	**0.07** (0.06)	30,505	**3.75** (2.98)
Most affluent 10%	2063	430	**0.06** (0.05)	23,040	**3.10** (2.67)
Total	**21,319**	**7720**	**0.10** (0.07)	**381,865**	**4.76** (3.88)

Source: Permanent and fixed period exclusions in England: 2016/17

There is some embarrassment about the figures in both tables. Firstly, in terms of attainment, going from the poorest to the most affluent, the scores rise almost without a blip. A worrying feature is that the gap between rich and poor grows as they pass through the schooling system. At 16, the gap is considerable; twice the proportion in the top 10 per cent reach the benchmark compared with the bottom 10 per cent. It is especially embarrassing that the same measures over a number of years have yielded the same results. It would be no surprise if there were no change in 2018. Amazingly, the statistics show exclusions, fixed period or permanent, display the same ratio: least affluent excluded at twice the rate of the most affluent. No surprises there. Both have been called a scandal. Our schools system, they say, should be dealing with this, in concert with other levels of policy making, and the academy system cannot be expected to make a difference in this area, even if we claim that we do and will.

Privatised services for the most needy?

There has always been the double bind in terms of 'we can do it better' and 'no, we don't kick up a fuss about needing more money'. Well we do, but behind the scenes, which makes it look like we are complicit in all this cost cutting – and we are. A challenge for us privatisers is not to let too many things go belly-up. People reason that a public service, which, let's face it, benefits us all, needs to be funded to an appropriate level. Not all services are of equal importance. More telling is the problem of those parts of the service which are super expensive and the academy sector can deliver on these more cheaply. It is not for the academy sector to deal with those social challenges from obesity, to stabbing to youthful relationships (teen pregnancies), county lines and so on.

Some 'client groups' are difficult to work successfully with. The low attainers and the semi-delinquent are amongst them. The renationalisation of the probation service[38] has done the private sector no favours as it was claimed not to be meeting its targets even after extra money was thrown at it. Academies must ensure that they are seeming to do the right thing by the most challenging cohorts even when they are not.

Looking at the parallels with education, the probation service manages more than a quarter of a million offenders in England and under a programme known as *Transforming Rehabilitation*, 35 probation trusts were replaced in 2014 by the National Probation Service (NPS) and 21 privately-owned community rehabilitation companies (CRCs). Even if high-risk individuals were supervised by the NPS, it left a lot of work for the CRCs, which they could not manage effectively and the whole rushed and inadequately funded system fell apart. The system for all these vulnerable and challenging people, if it fails, can affect us all in terms both of crime and of the cost of further sentencing and recall to prison. It is a bit of a conundrum for the quasi-private sector, priding itself as it does on efficiency and cost cutting, to handle that small part of the business that is getting ever more expensive but for which there is minimal credit. Grammar schools get top results, along with privates, but they and MATs are not in the business of social engineering or altering structures in society.

While schools were part of the cosy local authority set-up, they could rightly claim to be doing a job for the community. They could own up to difficulties and expect both sympathy and some money to follow. If you have set yourself up as a business, claiming to do the same job better for less, and make a profit, and pay top people big salaries, and IF you fail some groups, and those groups are predictable and expensive, then the structure is in trouble. Bad publicity about *not* coping with special needs, about *off-rolling* or more honestly *excluding* challenging young people will give the message that we cannot do the job of educating those from poorer neighbourhoods. THEN WE SHOULD NOT BE IN THE BUSINESS AT ALL, or only the independent or grammar school sectors.

If the wheels come off the outsourcing, sub-contracting and out-and-out privatising there will be uproar and we will face the spectre of renationalisation and all that blethering about public money for public services under public control again. Heaven help us if they get decent managers who can do the sums, work with the politicians, draw on research, manage hype similar to the academy sector, win public support and acquire and allocate the funding to meet effectively the needs of the most needy. Then, it would be like the third way had failed and we would suffer the ignominy of having dragged the system too far into the private sector rather than working, in a balanced way, with both national and local government.

There are enough scandals in the academy sector and we can

laugh off most with a joke about bad eggs and rogues everywhere, but other privatised utilities and services are feeling the heat and this could presage the end of the good money-making times for edu-preneurs. Therefore, we need to sort out how to deal with low attainment and disproportionate levels of exclusion in low socio-economic groups

A solution to managing the tough bits

This is where the business nous comes into its own. We have to accept that we cannot satisfy all the people all of the time and that means not satisfying some sections of the clientele, and we know which sections they are. We have to think out of the box, fly a kite or two, but make the books balance and keep our top people, and some of those in the tier below, happy.

There are two equally important parts to this solution and you have to get both parts right. The first strategy is to *claim repeatedly and loudly that you are dedicated to a good education and high standards for all*. Shout about how you are FOR the special needs kiddies and the trouble-makers and the slovenly, couldn't care less, non-aspirational. Really, really push this as they will not believe you if you do not claim this as amongst your foremost goals. Ensure that the minister says it, the heads of agencies say it and mock those who would dare suggest that you are not putting resources into these areas generously. Do not falter in your advocacy of the rights of the special education needs and disability (SEND) children; equally, give loads of examples of the ways in which you are accommodating those at risk of exclusion and equally again demonstrate how you are using the Pupil Premium Grant to good effect.

Behind all this is the core business, achievement. The over-riding standards emphasis has been with us for decades. It is a narrow tradition that goes back a long way, but if we start with the Department for Children, Schools and Families (DCSF) 2009 document, *Your child, your schools, our future: building a 21st century schools system*, with chapters headed: 'preparing children for the challenges of the 21st century; every school: excellent teaching and the extra help each child needs; every school in partnerships because no school can do it alone; every school improving, strong accountability and rapid intervention when needed etc', we can sign up to all that.

Michael Gove in 2011 refers to his 2010 White Paper where: 'we took a tougher line on underperformance than ever before by raising the floor standard for secondary schools to 35 per cent of pupils achieving five GCSEs at A*–C including English and maths' as well as recognising, from the Wolf report on vocational education, that 'the introduction of large numbers of vocational equivalents to the GCSE performance tables in 2004 has led to widespread gaming of qualifications', so he put a stop to that. That is fine also and fits with the more focussed, no frills curriculum academies favour.

Nick Gibb, speaking in 2016, said, amongst other things, 'Since coming into government in 2010, our reforms to the A-levels, GCSEs, and the national curriculum have focussed on bringing a new level of academic rigour to English state schooling. And central to this mission has been elevating knowledge to become a central component of a good school education.' Yes, academic rigour, elevating knowledge, good school education. We are dedicated to all that.

The second strategy is to actually do the opposite and kick out or restrict entry to SEND children, avoid where possible the 'disadvantaged' and remove from your school the unruly or even the unwanted. Do this with a certain amount of caution. Do not get found out. We can stand a certain amount of embarrassment but we do not want academies to be even smirkingly referred to as schools only for the good kids.

The second solution is for academies themselves to laud their credentials of low exclusions and succeeding with pupils from deprived backgrounds, while *finding ways to limit the intake of, or manage the departure of, poor pupils, SEND pupils and behaviourally challenging pupils.* A key ingredient is to deny, and deny again, that this is happening despite whatever evidence they can throw at you.

Our politicians are clear about the everlasting belief that education can cure all social ills. Michael Gove feels deeply about the plight of the poor, 'the scandal which haunts my conscience is the plight of those students from the poorest backgrounds, in the poorest neighbourhoods, in our poorest-performing schools who need us to act if their right to a decent future is to be guaranteed' and 'my moral purpose in Government is to break the lock which prevents children from our poorest families making it' acknowledging that, 'As a nation, we still do not do enough to extend the liberating power of a great education to the poorest.'

Nick Gibbs, too, has high expectations that 'Our education system should be an engine of social mobility, extending opportunity to every young person.' Teresa May, as prime minister in 2017, was set on, 'reforming our schools and ensuring that every child has the opportunity to thrive in a post-Brexit Britain'.

Academy chains and individual academies can do their part with appropriate window dressing. As just one example, Ark MAT tells the public that: 'Ark is an international charity, transforming lives through education. We exist to give every young person, regardless of background, a great education.'

The balance is between saying that each academy is open, welcomes all and is signed up to the 'dream' that all politicians have that education can work wonders for even the pupils from the poorest circumstances. We must not push this too far as you will get parents with special needs children beating a path to the door of the local Fair Access Panel which will suggest your school takes the newly arrived EAL (English as an Additional Language) young person, or the adolescent who has 'had to be moved on' from another secondary school. Talk the talk, as politicians do, present an image of welcome, but do all you can to manipulate your intake.

Structuring for (high) standards

Regardless of the hype and the rhetoric, what really counts in education in terms of reputation, inspections, local publicity are levels of attainment and behaviour. Select children well, and of course work hard with them while you have them, but be realistic about the biggest asset in achieving high grades which is family background. Look again at the graph and tables earlier in this chapter. Keep that to yourselves, but it should be there in the back of your mind when accepting applicants to your school.

Most satisfying from where the academy collective stands is the view of impotent protesters who still yearn for a comprehensive, inclusive, locally accountable, fully-funded, fun and games school curriculum. Eat your heart out CASE (Campaign for State Education), AAA (Anti Academies Alliance), Reclaim our Schools, Socialist Educational Association, with your miniscule memberships and even less influence, and never let the following quote be seen in any of your classrooms as was spotted in an LA school: 'Imagination is more important than knowledge' – Albert Einstein.

6. Screw the vocational curriculum and make it more 'scholarly'

Education for all

Education should encompass so-called high-status knowledge and skills and prepare young people to just live, to be, to know. Getting a job that is useful and pays a wage to live on is another thing. So, what do we do to make our schools complement home life and experience in the local community and help children and young people blossom into full, alert active citizens? Biology or bricklaying? Shakespeare or hairdressing? Algebra or caring for old people? There used to be choices and BTec vocational courses even overlapped with the academic courses to the extent that you could get FOUR A–C grade GCSE equivalents from your BTec courses until 2009. So where did it all go wrong? Or right, if you are one of those intellectual climbers who can discuss Shakespeare sonnets, and tell them from Webster's (who he?), but can't change a fuse, still less know how to get a demented mother looked after.

The National Curriculum was the first step, a monumental, amateur (nothing wrong with that) concoction that led the way to disciplining the education workforce and made learning more academic – that means 'better', doesn't it? – and less artisan, less common, less mucky, less low class.

Academies bear no blame for this development and the Labour government was not averse to tightening the academic grip and devaluing the practical. Academies have, however, gone with alacrity for the traditional, academic, formally assessed subjects.

The National Curriculum

It was possibly the most depressing moment in British education, when all schools were instructed in 1988 to start an INSET training day (all schools simultaneously) watching a presentation on video given by Kenneth Baker, the then Education Secretary. This set out the new National Curriculum that had been hastily developed. Some say it was by Oxford mates and some say on the back of a fag pack (can't be both, surely) at a government away-day. This was the beginning of the downward spiral to a narrow academic syllabus that, with increasing government pressure, would limit schools' ability to offer a wide-ranging curriculum that could encourage interest and develop the skills of all the pupils. The same Kenneth Baker later supported the establishment of CTCs (City Technology Colleges) that were meant to cater for the 14–18-year-olds who wished to pursue technical courses; exactly the areas of the curriculum that his National Curriculum caused to wither in the comprehensive schools. Many of these CTCs subsequently failed because they were used as 'dumping grounds' by schools anxious to lose the less academic 14-year-olds who would diminish their GCSE league table results. University Technical Colleges (UTCs) were much the same in aiming low and similarly failing; academy takeover was the only solution.

Reports abound about the greater time allocated to core subjects and those counting towards Attainment 8 and Progress 8, with arts, PE, drama and even PSHE and other 'frills', even breaks, reduced in length.

This narrowing of the curriculum is having consequences in the primary and even early-years sectors where, despite all the evidence that academics and researchers produce, nationally and internationally, pointing to the detrimental effects of such a process, schools are forced to spend increasing amounts of time teaching 'to the test' with many of the tests being of little or no value to pupil development. There is a lot of resistance to these developments being demonstrated with many teachers urging that there are more imaginative and flexible ways available to assess young people's learning. At secondary level, continuous assessment, so much better suited to some groups of learners, has been reduced to a minimal element.

Whatever happened to the practical and vocational curriculum?

Once there was the tri-partite system of grammar, technical and secondary modern schools. There was plenty of the technical and lots of vocational in the secondary moderns. The technical schools really morphed into the 'selective group' and status requirements set them on the same academic emphasis as the grammars. Curriculum content proceeded in a fairly unguided way right up to the imposition of the national curriculum in 1989. There had been the artificially created upsurge in interest, and funding, for something different from the Technical and Vocational Initiative (TVEI), sponsored by the Manpower Services Commission (MSC), and it gave a fillip to some chosen schools.

This had a relatively short life existing alongside the traditional curriculum from 1983 to 1997. After 14 years, it was felt that its impact had seeped into schools and it did not need to function as a separate curriculum track. Interestingly, it was a scheme much loved by Margaret Thatcher, Lord Young, who was a main instigator, and Sir Keith Joseph. All this is history but the impact was said to be lasting, if rather absorbed by BTEC and City and Guilds syllabuses and qualifications. It did give a certain modernity and even substantial teacher involvement in the actual interpretation of the scheme as implemented in their schools.

Three developments reshaped the curriculum and such vocational content as it contained during the early 2000s. Firstly, the decision by Ed Balls, the Labour Secretary of State for Education, that the benchmark for calculating attainment at 16 would be 5+ GCSEs at grades A*–C *which must include English and maths*. It was the maths that was the real killer and led some schools above benchmark results to halve. No matter that not even a mathematician can tell you what a C pass in maths student can do, that a D student cannot.

The second significant shift came with the 2011 Wolf review of vocational qualifications[39]. This put a stop to large numbers of vocational equivalents counting towards the GCSE performance tables, a trend that had been growing since 2004. Michael Gove saw this as leading to widespread gaming of qualifications. He saw the 4000 per cent rise in the number of such qualifications taken in just 6 years as testament to this. More than 3000 qualifications which thousands of students had been happily doing were to be disregarded leaving just 70. Attributing value to a City and Guilds level 2 diploma in horse care, worth four GCSEs in the league tables or a BTEC in fish husbandry, worth two GCSEs, a level 2 certificate in nail technology and a level 2 award in travel and tourism was just a joke. All were dropped and a more streamlined curriculum more suited to the modern age was introduced. Maybe it is a pity that some of the traditional craft and trade skills did not make it through because many of us are aware of how it is easier to find a historian than a bricklayer, or one that has been educated in a school in England. Anyway, 'Professor Wolf argues that we need a wholesale realignment of incentives' (Gove's Foreword to the report), but this may have altered school incentives to whack up their GCSE count. It has also removed educational and scholastic incentives for some young people who were never going to make it to the then benchmark of 5 A*–C including maths and English.

Admittedly, some of the vocational courses were extremely expensive, requiring specialist spaces and smaller class sizes and this was not the way government thinking was going. Also for most of the ministers and civil servants directing education, it was beyond their ken. Education as they experienced it would not have given over much time to banging in nails in the woodwork room and bathing dolls in child development lessons. And the idea of achieving qualifications in these 'pastimes' would not have appealed to many of their parents who were paying expensive fees for their children to gain access to the higher echelons of society and freeing up the parents to do more useful things with their time. (In many ways the study of child development would have undermined the whole idea of farming out parental responsibility to boarding schools.) This traditional view of education was 'good for us – it did us no harm – what's the problem?'

And so the national curriculum was imposed on state schools and an academic timetable replaced the broader offer that had been available and all young people were straightjacketed into it, whether it was suitable or not. Contrast this with Germany where a technical education is given equal status and where industrial innovation creates a more balanced economy less reliant on financial services. Building manufacturing capacity and a balanced economy requires 'a more active and purposeful state' according to the IPPR report, *Prosperity and Justice: A Plan for a New Economy*, just what you expect when funding for their Commission[40] was provided by the Friends Provident Charitable Foundation, the City of London Corporation, the Trade Unions Council, the GMB and the Transport Salaried Staffs' Association, all left-leaning and backward-looking. So that is one to dismiss.

The third nail in the vocational coffin was in 2012 when compulsory work experience was abolished and 14- to 16-year olds were no longer given the 2-week glimpse of a small part of the adulthood that awaited them. There were too many important demands from excessive exam preparations to allow time for this period of contemplating coming maturity and what a loss this was. We now have organisations like the Federation of Small Businesses lobbying for its return as it enabled their members to hire young people from harder-to-reach backgrounds and to aid their recruitment gaps. Education for life? – nonsense! – exams, exams, exams!

Where's Charlie? Where's Cheryl?

Charlie is the next-door neighbour to die for. He is an electrician by qualification, wonderfully adept at most practical tasks. He knows how to replace a tap or put together an IKEA jigsaw pack of furniture. But despite his City and Guilds certificates, he always defers to 'educated' people who read books and *The Guardian*. He, of course, was repairing computers long before most of us could play Rock-Man on our Commodore Vic 20s, but because of society's distorted view of intelligence and worth he has never fully appreciated his achievements and his value. If only he had spent more time studying the classics rather than taking apart his motorbike!

Cheryl is an angel. She is married with two children and does part-time work caring for an old couple for 3 hours a day. She is a delight to have around for Albert (82) and Doris (84). She chats away, sings, cleans and, without trying, entertains her elderly and ailing 'clients'. Professionally, she has an NVQ Level 3 in Adult Social Care and has attended workshops to make sure she caters for dietary and medical maintenance needs for the two old folk. She has that ability, partly learnt, to get them up, walking around and even feeling useful in the kitchen. She has no GCSE above a grade 4 to her name. As she says, it was not her 'thing'. But wow, what a worker and what a human being.

The idea that education must be broader and more inclusive is not for the academy sector to take on. Indeed, the academy sector is bent on narrowing and making more efficient the education provided. Vocational education and on-the-job training will have to come later. The public will not object to what is being done. They are loath to challenge the establishment. One hundred years after universal suffrage and two hundred years after the Enlightenment, our leaders still come from the same few public schools and Oxbridge and our state schools still ape their style of education. The public stay silent on the academisation project taking over their schools if it is done subtly and gradually with the proper respect shown to traditional knowledge.

The Blob says the way forward in relation to the vocational/ academic/cultural content of the curriculum is for governments of all persuasions to withdraw from interfering in the curriculum and for professional bodies to determine the needs of pupils, liaising with parents and other agencies, with governments providing the funding and leaving the electorate to determine whether or not a particular regime is providing adequately. That is half right, but don't leave it to teachers and their organisations, don't involve parents and once the academy movement is flying it will deliver to the politicians who have believed in the freedom that has been rightly granted.

Courses for horses

The major problem with all the self-expression and creativity is that it challenges the traditional order. Education in the 60s and 70s resulted in chaos – protests, strikes, young people thinking they had a right to influence and challenge the status quo – indeed Status Quo and their ghastly noise were typical of the rubbish produced, as were the kitchen sink dramas and films depicting ordinary people's lives and pointing to the need to change. Schools were even incorporating plays like *A Taste of Honey* by Shelagh Delaney and some dubious modern poets into the examination syllabus.

We need a workforce which is compliant, happy to view the latest Hollywood fantasy blockbuster as entertainment of the highest order, who try to pay their bills with ever-decreasing wages, that do not get ideas above their station and challenge those better suited to govern who are earning well and enjoying the finer things of life.

'We need educational experiences and learning opportunities which suit the full range of learners, which represent the culture as we know it and can enable a student to go forward to a useful work life, satisfying personal relationships and participation as a citizen', so it is said. This is lefty drivel – get them working wherever we need them and hope their school experience does not make them too uppity.

We may not be producing the work horses for the lower, and it must be said, declining echelons of the employment sector but manpower planning is for government to sort out. The agenda is clear. Core English, maths and science and some other straightforward courses from the bucket (Year 9 subject selections) to make a decent Attainment 8 score.

7. Pay the few much more and care much less

Diverting money to top executives and away from front line need?

Let us take this one head-on. In 2016, the claim was made that heads of taxpayer-funded independent chains are making claims that include fast cars, first-class travel and Marco Pierre White dining while schools struggle. The leaders of academy schools are spending taxpayers' money on luxury hotels, top-end restaurants, first-class travel, private health care and executive cars. How else do we attract the right people? If only people understood business, they would know that benefits trickle down as senior executives make wise decisions and allocate time and resources to the areas where you get best results.

Expense claims released under the Freedom of Information Act lay bare what critics claim is an extraordinary extravagance by some academy chain chief executives and principals, at a time when schools are struggling financially. The taxpayer, it is said, is paying Ian Cleland, he of the £180,000-a-year chief executive at Academy Transformation Trust, the cost of a leased XJ Premium Luxury V6 Jaguar car, nearly £3000 worth of receipts for servicing the car and the purchase of new tyres.

Cleland also spent £3000 of taxpayers' money on first-class rail travel, while dining expenses racked up on his taxpayer-funded credit card include a meal with other staff at Marco Pierre White totalling £471, and the Bank restaurant in Birmingham, at a cost £703.45.

Cleland announced in March that the Trust was looking to save £500,000 from its 21 schools in the Midlands and east of England and had asked staff to reapply for their jobs. 'The education sector is facing a number of significant financial challenges across the country with all schools, academies and multi-academy trusts being affected,' he said at the time. 'As a result, it is essential that we review our costs and consider where savings can be made, without impacting on the quality of education.'

Elsewhere in the country, thousands of pounds have been spent at top hotels and even rooms in luxury golf clubs by senior executives working for academy trusts. The public has also regularly funded first-class travel and poured money into taxi firms. The largest 40 academy trusts have spent more than £1m of public money on executive expenses since 2012.

The Paradigm Trust paid for CEO Amanda Phillips (deceased) to have broadband at her holiday home in France, even though she earned £195,354 a year.

Meanwhile, former education secretary Michael Gove's vision of a more market-led school system has materialised, in which multi-academy trusts have taken the place of local authorities and salary levels have soared within the management tier. More than half of the largest 50 chains pay their chief executives more than the prime minister (£143,000). Sir Daniel Moynihan, the chief executive of the high-performing Harris Federation, earns £395,000 a year, but that was 2 years ago and it exceeds £400,000 now. Lois Reed, one of only three women in this top bracket, had a salary of £270,000 in 2016/17 but has left (June 2018), partly because the disparity with her earning nearly £200,000 more than any other employees.

It is unfortunate that only three of those in the academies rich list are women, but the equality demand comes below the business skill set and temperament requirements. It is a minor area for the sector to work on and it is noted that the proportion of females in these top leadership jobs is 15 per cent, while the proportion of secondary heads who are female is around 35 per cent. The chief executive of the Aspirations Academies Trust, which runs 14 schools, pays its chief executive and founder, Steve Kenning, a total package of £225,000, while his wife, Paula

Top 20 Highest Paid Trust Bosses (Schools Week[41], 1 March, 2019)

CHIEF EXECUTIVE	TRUST	MINIMUM TOTAL PAY 2017-18	MINIMUM TOTAL PAY 2016-17	Academy numbers June 2019
Dan Moynihan	Harris Federation	£440,000	£440,000	47
Julian Drinkall	Academies Enterprise Trust	£290,000	£264,000	62
Kevin Satchwell	Telford City Technology College	£270,000	£270,000	1
John Tomasevic	Nova Education Trust	£260,000	£260,000	15
Colin Hall	Holland Park	£260,000	£245,000	1
Lois Reed	Transforming Lives Education Trust	£250,000	£270,000	2
Jon Coles	United Learning Trust	£240,000	£240,000	72
Lucy Heller	ARK Schools	£236,000	£237,500	38
Steve Lancashire	REAch2 Academy Trust	£230,000	£240,000	55
Adrian Reed	Boston Witham Academies Federation	£230,000	£220,000	8
Andy Goulty	Rodillian MAT	£225,000	£220,000	5
Simon Beamish	Leigh Academies Trust	£220,000	£180,000	23
Hamid Patel	Star Academies	£220,000	£210,000	28
Dayo Olukoshi	Brampton Manor Trust	£220,000	£200,000	2
Patricia Davies	Silver Birch Academy	£220,000	£210,000	4 (closed)
John Murphy	Oasis Community Learning	£210,000	£200,000	52
Steve Kenning	Aspirations Academy Trust	£210,000	£205,000	14
John Townsley	Gorse Academies Trust	£210,000	£200,000	11
Roger Leighton	Partnership Learning	£210,000	£210,000	12
Steve Morrison	Kingfisher Foundation	£210,000	£210,000	2

Kenning, receives £175,000 as executive principal and founder. And as the salaries have shot up, the so-called related-party transactions – where companies with close links to directors of academy trusts are paid for services to those trusts – have also multiplied. It is to be repeated: there is nothing wrong with this.

As an example, Russ Quaglia, the American who co-founded the Aspirations Academy Trust (AAT), was contracted through his US-based Quaglia Institute to deliver 15 days of training and consultancy to AAT on themes to do with 'school voice and aspirations' at a cost of almost £90,000. The trust claimed that it had his services at reduced fees and assured the regulator that it was abiding by the no-profit rule governing such transactions. AAT gave an account of all the expenses – flight, hotels, meals – and provided evidence that Dr Quaglia's daily rate was usually higher.

AAT also gave an account of Quaglia's top-of-the-range staff and student surveys which cost an additional $20,000 a year.

A spokesman for AAT said:

Dr Quaglia is a highly respected figure in international education...in high demand around the world...grateful for his commitment to the trust and to improving the aspirations and life chances of our students. The amounts that we pay to the institute are openly disclosed in our accounts, have been assessed as being 'at cost' in line with Department for Education rules, are audited by independent external auditors and full information has been disclosed to the department, who have not raised any concerns.[42]

The Department for Education says that such transactions 'can save money' but that they investigate and will take 'swift action' where there is cause for concern. Margaret Hodge MP, former chair of the Commons Public Accounts Committee, said that the checks and balances in the academy system were not robust enough and that if organisations are getting involved in schools for the public good, then they should not be making money out of it. Intriguing that none of this stuff ever comes out because of the regulators discovering things; it is unbelievably soft-touch regulation, such as educational entrepreneurs could only have dreamt of.

Shadow chancellor John McDonnell MP said: 'The Tories have shown that when it comes to most people, they aren't afraid to take in-work benefits or public services off us. But when it comes to the bosses of their failing academy programme, no expense is spared.' Mr McDonnell knows nothing.

In 5 years the number of academies has grown from 600 to more than 5000, while the regulator's staffing numbers have collapsed. The risk analysis division of the Education Funding Agency (EFA), that looks at the finances of academy trusts, dealt with 125 per cent more financial returns in 2014–15 than the previous year, despite having 20 per cent fewer staff.

'There are huge amounts of public money being shovelled around in the schools system, and unless the ESFA ups its game, plenty of unscrupulous people out there will help themselves,' said Margaret Hodge when she was Chair of the Public Accounts Committee.

A spokesman for ATT said:

Restaurant expenses were related to events for staff, teachers and principals and not personal use. Ian is provided with a lease vehicle as part of his remuneration package. The cost of maintaining this vehicle is paid for by the trust. Ian's role requires significant, regular travel throughout the regions where our academies are based, hence the maintenance costs, including tyres and vehicle health checks.

Cuts, cuts, cuts

Since 2010 the need for austerity and balancing the nation's books has been the main concern of the government. And quite right too! No one should live beyond their means and, when governments do, it results in indulgence and encourages laziness.

If we look at education before 2010, we see an expansion of 'special needs' provision and a ridiculous explosion of support staff in schools, where old-fashioned discipline which enabled a teacher, working alone, to contain classes was abandoned in favour of understanding each pupil's needs and, very often, this involved the employment of one-to-one support and classroom assistants, most of whom spent their time wiping noses or putting up displays. It was a sheer waste of money and time, in most cases, to suggest that these pupils needed extra provision. What they needed was the satisfaction that comes with success and this is only achieved through hard work and discipline, things that sadly they often didn't see exhibited in their home lives. (Put a few ex-army teachers in front of them – that'll sort them out! and if it doesn't, off-roll them so they don't bring down the school's league table position.)

Another area that also needed addressing was the amount of time pupils were spending on hobby subjects like the arts and sport and 'practical' areas of the curriculum that require expensive equipment and for 'health and safety' reasons smaller classes. If only we could keep pupils at their desks, the financial savings would be tremendous although we now have to install laptops on the desks to ensure that children are employable when they become part of the workforce. If young people need to indulge in creative areas then that can be provided through extra-curricular activities that teachers will be 'encouraged' to provide even though most of them will be too down-trodden by the increasing pressures to improve their exam results to have the energy to offer them.

But it's not just about schools. Many of the activities that keep young people engaged used to be accessible in youth clubs, many of which were attached to schools and were funded by the local authority. Another area for 'austerity' to **decimate.** Let the voluntary sector take this on and so reduce expenditure. This would only work if there was sufficient capacity and that there were not so many faith-based organisations as they are less attractive than community-based clubs. But austerity must be the priority and if we have more young people joining gangs and killing each other, usually in drug-related scenarios, then so be it. And to suggest that the reduction in police numbers and particularly the loss of the ward level community teams has anything to do with the increase in stabbings is just ridiculous. (However, there are lots of examples of police support officers pre-empting gang disturbances and vendettas or having vital information post-events. Sadly, most of this expertise and experience has been lost since the cuts.) And anyway, most of these incidents happen in communities that are far removed from the constituencies of the majority of current government ministers and MPs. And, in addition, if the 'do–gooders' had benefited from a 'real' education they would know that teenagers and young people have always formed gangs and stabbed each other – remember Romeo and Juliet!

The academies programme will deal with many of these difficulties. Most young people will learn to be un-questioning and so dedicated to the real function of education – passing exams and behaving like good citizens – that they will have no time or energy to indulge in extra-curricular activities, positive or negative For those with special needs, as many as possible should be off-loaded to the increasingly depleted local authorities' provision. Alternatively, reduce the support available in academies to such an extent that they will become a serious threat to our success story so we'll quietly suggest a bit of home-schooling in the run-up to public examinations and tests. After all the majority of these pupils are never going to make much of themselves so a few more months on the streets will be good preparation for a NEET (15 per cent) life living on decreasing benefits and increasing temptation. NEETs are Not in Education Employment or Training.

For examples of the trend in academies to downgrade special needs provision one needs to look no further than Leigh Academies Trust which took over a school in Greenwich and renamed it Halley Academy. The irony is that the school had been famous as the first purpose-built comprehensive in the country – Kidbrooke School.

Within a year of the take-over, the school with 160 pupils with extra support needs or disabilities tried to make 17 of the teaching assistants redundant while the trust's chief executive, Simon Beamish, was paid more than £220,000 for 2018. Another example is the head, who was appointed in London on the strength of having turned round a school in Portsmouth, who was so unpopular that she left after a couple of terms of trying to academise the school and it was then discovered that her success on the south coast had been in the large part due to radically reducing the school roll, mostly by a drastic reduction in its special needs intake. Success with the easy kids? – It seems to be a pattern! Education for all? – so unfashionable!

For parents of children with special needs it has become increasingly difficult because where do you turn if you feel your child is being short-changed? Local accountability has gone and to challenge a MAT – where do you start? They are unelected and have no legal responsibility to educate all children. Your only chance of redress is to go to the District Schools Commissioner and then the Secretary of State – well good luck with that! Children with special needs are a drag on an outstanding school's success story and despite the extra funding that follows these children they frequently don't get the full benefit. Success is easy to measure – SATs, GCSE and A level results – ultimately every school's headlines! If some children are left behind – what's the problem? They are a drain on limited resources and will probably never produce at the level a successful society needs to compete in the global economy. 'There is no such thing as society,' as one famous (infamous?) woman stated but that is truly where we are. She, also, as prime minister in 1983, at a cabinet meeting, suggested that the NHS could be dismantled and was fortunately persuaded away from the proposal. But the legacy lives on and in starving health and education of sufficient funds the tactic has now become more subtle. If the services do not come up to scratch then people will cease to support them and vote with their wallets to increase private provision. After 9 years of austerity the books have not been balanced – nowhere near – and education is being starved of adequate resources and being opened up to privatisers and profit seekers who want to put competition above education. Society is a thing of the past and the food banks and the widening gap between the haves and the have-nots are just the price we have to pay for the progress of unfettered capitalism.

The care agenda

Revelations of the high salaries of MAT CEOs comes at a difficult time when they is juxtaposed with funding being cut in so many areas. Moving to a business mentality, thoroughly appropriate to state education, requires some alignment to the wider salary expectations in the private sector. Bankers, CEOs or a range of service companies receive high salaries and one key difference is that in the academies sector, in receipt of government money to do a job and do it well, there are no share options and few bonuses. MATs across the country are not paying excessive salaries and the letter demanding explanations from Lord Agnew is, to be frank, an insult.

In education, there are costs which are high for additional support for SEND children and for inclusion and isolation facilities. It is simply naive to suggest, as too many have done, that there is a link between the high salary for a CEO and having to make five TAs redundant. You may as well say that poor people struggling to pay gas, electricity or water bills would have lower prices if the CEOs took less and if dividends to shareholders were lower. The world does not run like that and these linkages are spurious, if not mischievous.

The heart tugging care agenda in general is not our business and if our goal is high attainment levels for those in the schools system capable of it, then we should be absolutely fixated on it.

The care agenda should be almost totally separated from the work, and indeed, mission, of academies. It is difficult enough fielding the challenges and charges about SEND and exclusions without seeing wider issues related to how the society we are creating is leading also to increases in rough sleepers, food banks, child poverty, even longevity. There is the claim that this is neo-liberalism and global capitalism, realities that are indeed driving the popularity of states choosing to privatise education and perhaps these sad developments are the inevitable consequences, collateral damage, if you like. There may be casualties for the greater good and the casualties are the usual group: poor people.

The attainment agenda is the one academies, individually and collectively, will win on. Restricting numbers of SEND pupils will be helpful, in that regard, as will a bit of judicious off-rolling. A bigger problem is the continuing low attainment of those growing up in more deprived circumstances. As set out earlier, avoid letting them in to a degree, but also some academies have really good figures for PPG (pupil premium grant) pupils' attainment. Academies must flag up these successes with named schools and the numbers that go with their results.

In a public relations landscape, academy senior management and trustees need to navigate the message to the public and politicians that the academy movement believes in education for all. However, claiming to have a lot of SEND pupils or that you manage behaviourally challenging youngsters well does not necessarily show the institution in a positive light. Taking that theme further, any claim on the impressive attainment of pupil premium or free school meals pupils again sends a compromised message. Will parents want to send their children to a place where there are SO many of these young people, even if they do well. Let LA schools take as much credit as they like in this area, but the academy sector can just concentrate on the overall attainment rates at Key Stage 2 and Key Stage 4.

Of course, academies must give every impression that they care for every child and every sort of child but the efficient achievement (creation?) of an impressive end product depends as much on the quality of input materials as on the skill of the 'manufacturer'. That applies as much to pupils as to meat pies, a Ford car or a professional football team and another agricultural saying about sow's ear and silk purse might be appropriate.

8. Out-source slickly with relaxed attitudes to friends and relations 'winning' contracts − sailing close to the wind?

A winner for sure

The bulk of a school's budget goes on staff, maintenance of equipment and buildings, and teaching materials. Something like 10 per cent of the budget is discretionary, or at least not directly allocated to a provider. This is a fairly big opportunity for the entrepreneurs, and for speed to meet needs, contracts can be let with minimal fuss. We should be warned that if through speed and efficiency we cross the line, there could be problems − big or small. No one is waiting for the Grenfell Tower of education failure through cronyism and poor regulation. However, evidence of strains and problems are emerging but, like the public relations effort mentioned earlier exonerating academies from fault or shortcomings, these are robustly denied, as business people in expansion mode would do.

Business acumen ahead of commitment

There was a time, not long ago, in a rather relaxed professional environment, when teachers went into education with that mythical sense of dedication and in the full knowledge that it was not a route to wealth but they would be rewarded by earning a reasonable salary and, if they did enough years, a respectable pension plus the satisfaction of doing a worthwhile job in a reasonably secure profession. 'Oh, happy days,' some say. These lucky, contented souls also felt that they had the opportunity to contribute to the development of 'education' by being listened to and respected as professionals. It was not that long ago when decision-making in a school would result from consultation and, in many establishments, a democratic process would help to determine the direction departments would pursue. Sometimes parents were consulted and children, even young children. This was done partly in the quaint belief that wisdom can be found in the strangest of places and democracy is anyway a 'good thing'. That is a strange view of the world looking back with emphasis put on people being valued and respected. School management would not see this as a way to get a job done with maximum efficiency.

It was a La La Land where discussions were said to take place over whether or not some subjects in secondary schools should be examined at all, or whether the imposition of formal exams would limit the excitement and creativity that were intrinsic to those subjects. All of this was possible under local education management which exerted overall control of budgets and standards and was the employer of all education staff, both teachers and ancillary workers. It was a time that coincided with a period when professional educators had a say and could contribute to the debate on curriculum and assessment. There were national agreements over pay and conditions, no one made a fortune but most felt a sense of involvement in a vital public service and gained satisfaction from a shared purpose. Of course, none of this worked. This system, if that is what it was, cannot take the credit for those generations of pupils who went on to enable this country to be a powerhouse of creativity.

The new philosophy eased its way into education, the philosophy of efficiency and its family member – ruthlessness. In 2018, diverse organisations are running schools which prioritise attracting talented educators who will take on the tough job of chief executive of a MAT. It necessarily involves earning as much as (no, more than) the prime minister but requires a willingness to drive staff, remove dross and undermine those long fought-for pay and conditions for most employees of their trust. These are the role models of today, reshaping education content, processes and products and will be models that pupils look up to. 'Public service' is still embedded in the new philosophy but harder edged, more determined and, ultimately, more effective.

These new style organisations are growing in number and influence, consolidating their independence from LAs, enjoying their favoured standing with the DfE and exploiting the reduced public scrutiny and accountability. There is no limit to the outsourcing of work from clerical duties to repairs and staff development. Contracts being awarded without tendering, family and friends of family being given work without checks and due diligence, sometimes of questionable quality and staff being appointed occasionally without the requisite qualifications or experience. This is speedy management and there have been some 'issues', it cannot be denied: charges of cronyism, misuse of public money, overly generous 'expenses' and related-party deals. We can manage the fall-out from this and while the government happily denigrates teachers and the declining old-style educational establishment as the *Blob*, you have a recipe for a 'free for all' where schools can employ non-qualified teachers and chief executives of MATs can promise all kinds of promotions and advances to compliant staff and make life impossible for those who challenge the new structures. Examples of the new thinking displayed by recent government ministers at the Department for Education were proposals to encourage ex-military personnel to go into schools because their sense of discipline was just what pupils needed. Indeed, one government minister proposed establishing CCFs (Combined Cadet Forces) in all secondary schools. Just what the country needs – even more young people trained in the use of weapons – and not just knives. Another suggestion was that graduates with the highest degrees/grades should be persuaded to take up teaching. There's nothing wrong with high-flyers entering the profession but maybe something wrong with the concept that the higher the degree the better the teacher you will make. To be fair and broad-minded, some people make good teachers without the highest grades, and CCFs were established to provide officers for the First World War; even today, it is best to be prepared!

These ideas come from politicians who generally have little understanding of the majority of state schools, the background of most of their pupils and the fundamental basis upon which good teaching depends: the ability to form relationships with staff and between pupils. This is unsurprising when the background and educational experiences of most legislators are taken into account. Most of the politicians and civil servants who occupy influential positions in the Department for Education have come from privileged educational establishments and even those who were state educated experienced the best on offer and have little experience of the challenges and achievements of schools in more deprived circumstances. There is a need to create and embed an education system which fosters high achievement along narrow lines and that is what academies are (or should be) about. This is best left to even out-of-touch politicians rather than to the education experts – the Blob.

Relationships, relationships, relationships

Some angry, old-fashioned people cry out, 'When will the bastards comprehend the fundamentals of "education"?' *It's about relationships, stupid*, but it is about relationships of a particular sort. The hierarchy needs to be recognised, compliance with the agreed curriculum plan is a must and the zero-tolerance discipline policy must be implemented to the letter. Within that the billion-pound public education sector is great to toy with and exploit and relate together as a unified team.

State education does a magnificent job in general despite attempts to starve it of sufficient support and resources. Such cut-backs were tried with the NHS (National Health Service) but such was the public's reaction to many of the cuts, money has had to be found to reverse some changes, like the closure of some A & E departments. We must try to ensure the electorate are not made angry about these cuts and the dismantling of the state education system. There is no way we will budge until the voters insist that these changes are reversed and we are forced to return to a more democratic and child-centred system. Given time and the rate of privatisation, enough sensible citizens may have jumped on the bandwagon of what some people see as pure greed, corruption and dodgy dealing and eventually become stakeholders in the local multi-academy trust or free school.

It was once unusual, but now is entirely appropriate, to use the title *chief executive officer* in the realm of school education, and to give them massive power. Nick Osborne, CEO of the Maritime Trust with seven primary schools in south-east London and Kent (with more to come), persuaded Brooklands School to convert with the argument that the LA money would not be sufficient to maintain an outstanding school. 'Better to convert'. Three years down the line, staff and existing governors were concerned at planned changes to many of the safeguards that the original governors had written into the transfer conditions. An ex-local authority governor who had opposed transfer was asked: *What can we do about it?* The answer was 'nothing!' Having left the local authority and with the transfer of the assets and staff to the MAT, there was nowhere to turn when the trust decided to 'refresh the governance'. The chair and many of the governors resigned and there was no democratic avenue to pursue. The CEO's salary increased significantly year on year while at the same time he tried to persuade two valued office staff at Brooklands School to take a 30 per cent pay cut or redundancy[43], resulting in many parents being up in arms about their chief executive's exercise of such autocratic rule, as they saw it. They felt powerless to influence him. Too quick, Nick. Slow down or you risk giving everyone in the academy sector a bad name.

Academies are in the clear and on to a winner free to make those necessary and ultimately beneficial adjustments. There is nothing local people can do. Local opposition is powerless. It is too late. It has gone. It shows that opponents have to act fast, and academies and MATs have shown that they act faster.

Until legislation is passed, there is no way for a MAT, or its constituent schools, to return to the local authority but, of course, it can be absorbed by, or *rebrokered* into, a larger MAT, which will take it even further away from local accountability and parents and into the privatised, results-focussed paradise of academy-world.

It is best not to mention recent revelations (BBC's *Panorama*, 25 March 2019) etc. about the inflation of test and exam results, through pressure put on staff in certain MATs to cheat. But it is irresistible to list scandals. The academy sector has to own these, but they are small in number beside the huge progress being made.

- The *high salary levels* which everyone has talked about (see table in Chapter 7).
- *Kinsley Academy* less than 3 years old as an academy within the Wakefield City Academies Trust, judged 'Good' in January 2015, has seen standards and parent satisfaction plummet[44]. As Kinsley Primary School, it had served this rural, former mining community in West Yorkshire for over 100 years. It has now, with a name change, re brokered into Waterton Academy Trust.
- *Wakefield City Academies Trust* was a high-profile failure in 2015 mired in related-party transactions and accused of 'asset stripping' after transferring millions of pounds of the schools' savings to its own accounts before withdrawing in 2017 and dumping its 21 schools.
- *Lord Nash* was a schools minister from 2013 to 2017, during which time he chaired Future Academies academy chain which is accountable to the government department he helped to run.
- *Lord Agnew* founded the Inspiration Trust academy chain

in 2012, which in 2019 had 14 schools in East Anglia. He chaired the DfE's academies board from 2013, which involved oversight of the work of the regional schools commissioners who had oversight of Inspiration.

- *The Lilac Sky Schools Academy Trust* is forced to give up its nine schools. Its accounts reveal that it used public funding to pay consultants more than £1000 a day even as it was drawing on emergency public funding.

- The *Perry Beeches Academy Trust*, once praised by David Cameron as 'a real success story', gave up its five schools after reports of financial mismanagement. The trust paid an additional salary of £120,000 over 2 years to its former chief executive on top of his £80,000 annual salary[45].

- *Bright Tribe* made false claims for public money, around half a million pounds, for Whitehaven Academy in Cumbria, for building work never done to the standard it was costed at or left unfinished, while Colchester Academy in the same trust received £566,000 for work done which was independently assessed at only £60,000. And there were breaches of rules over payments to trustees. And there's more. Mr Dwan, founder of Bright Tribe, through his lawyers, denies everything[46]. As you would.

- The *TBAP academy chain* got it in the neck when a Harlow alternative provision free school head teacher turned whistleblower and charged that the finances had been appallingly managed and staff redundancies meant the school was no longer safe, catering as it did for some of the most challenging young people.

- Lord O'Shaughnessy launched *Floreat Education Academies (FEAT)* and it was praised by the PM in 2016. In September 2019 it was handing over its remaining two primary schools, but that is after receiving big money for proposed free school developments: Floreat Colindale (£120,000) and Floreat Southall (£120,000) and a further payment to Southall College (750,000) for costs incurred in relation to the latter. Neither free school opened. In 2015, Floreat received £124,000 to run a 'virtue and development programme' and questions were raised about £100,000 paid to O'Shaughnessy's Mayforth Consulting for services to the trust.

Sailing close to the wind is OK, if you are not found out, and maybe it will not do any damage to those high and mighty lords. The academisation movement could do with fewer of these escapades surfacing. There are more, but journalists would be wise to hold back for legal reasons. To be sure, the academy sector and its associated services are ripe for redirecting funds and benefitting friends and relations.

The 'relationships' which headed this section were about relationships with pupils and with parents, about professional relationships and even connections with one's morality and public service goals. Unfortunately, the academy narrative sometimes slips into rumour of graft and misuse of public funds. It is beyond stupid for people to equate a CEO's £150,000 or more salary with three or four extra teachers, or five or six teaching assistants in front of children in classrooms. CEOs' expertise and experience in turning schools around must never be under-valued.

An on-line post from the school desk of an uppity sixth-former reads as follows: 'I started a petition[47] about the CEO of the trust mis-using funding vis-à-vis a company set up to provide services to the MAT. My petition read – "Hold former *Education for the 21st Century Trust* (E21C) CEO Paul Murphy to account for off-payroll payments totalling £145,006".'[48] The petition was signed by 570 people. This funding over several years invoiced by Paul Murphy's personal services company for 'CEO services to the academy trust' would be on top of the salary Mr Murphy received for the day job, circa £125,000. It was not all going into his pocket, of course, but he was sole director of SPHA Ltd. The MAT could have sorted it out if left to its own devices, but this is what we have to contend with.

Getting wealthy is fine but getting caught out like this is just plain unintelligent and makes life difficult for the rest of the academisers. Students like this are becoming all too common and they need a talking to about their place and how adults are to be left to deal with adult things. There are too many young people getting above themselves, all copying Greta Thunberg, perhaps.

9. Promote lean national oversight by minimalist governmental agencies

Look back in wonder

Up to 2010, under the Labour government, schools were weighed down with direction and National Strategies and guidance documents. There was an excess of those 'experienced' people employed by the LA to support and advise schools in that gentle, respectful, old-style way. These advisers and officers were there to be supportive of schools, but there was also a fairly robust, if sometimes irksome, compliance role. If things went wrong or correct procedures were not followed, whether for recruitment, staff disciplinaries, admissions, exclusions and complaints, they were there to follow up. What a pain. Academies have freed themselves from (almost) all of that.

As for documentation since that time, Michael Gove dealt with it the instant he took up his post, reporting with justifiable pride that, 'freedom is proving an unstoppable driver of success' and he was:

> working hard to increase freedom for all our schools [by] reducing central government prescription for all schools to make heads' and teachers' lives easier and give them the space to focus on what really matters;
> reams of FMSIS (Financial Management Standard in Schools) forms gone;
> Performance Management guidance cut by three-quarters.
> capability procedures simplified.
> Ofsted framework slimmed down.
> Behaviour and bullying guidance cut from 600 pages to 50[49].

Other procedures were simplified, most significantly for complaints. The government's answer to the sweeping away of so-called democratic accountability is that parents and others can now appeal to the Regional Schools Commissioner (RSC), the Educational and Skills Funding Agency (ESFA), Ofsted or even the Department for Education. The convenience and irony of this lean structure is that there are very few staff employed at these levels to deal with complaints and difficulties and the few in situ are very removed from the local area. One RSC for part of the London area oversees schools from the Isle of Wight to Kent in addition to the metropolitan area. There is no way that these few staff have an understanding of the diversity of local issues or the time to deal with them, which is very much the way academisers want it, especially as it succeeds in putting off most people who would complain. Academies are both free of regulation and have little to fear from the minimal enforcement capability that is available should they transgress. Ombudsman and judicial review were both expected to be a back-up when normal administrative procedures fail, and they can be expensive. Many local authority education departments have hung on doggedly to advisory staff, but academies do not need them and if they come to talk over some issue, we can run rings round them – even ban them from the premises if they overstep the mark.

It is interesting to note that despite MATs selling themselves as better able to fund schools this is not the case. Pupils are funded at the same rate in all state schools and interestingly MATs etc generally top-slice 5 per cent of schools' budgets for their administrative costs whereas local authorities usually top-slice between 0.5 and 1.0 per cent. The extra money that appears to be available to MATs etc comes partly from downgrading salaries or employing younger, cheaper staff. Some of the 5 per cent top-sliced enables chief executives and senior staff to have appropriate salaries and benefits that would not be available under local/national agreements. To get the best, you have to pay top dollar, and don't they just.

It is not difficult to see why these new arrangements are attractive to a new breed of 'educationalists' and to see how the freedom is more fitting for this new educational era. More power and less supervision coupled with salaries more in keeping with junior bankers is what talent deserves. Public service is still there, but some way down the list and the burden of local accountability has been rightly obliterated.

Free schools were a maverick arrival further eroding the ability of local authorities to plan and supervise education in their counties, metropolitan areas and boroughs. Free schools were allowed to establish themselves in areas where, often, there was no shortage of school places and this was something of a challenge for the LA which had still a responsibility for the planning of school provision, but this apparent chaos is a small price to pay for diversity, choice, competition and freedom. Free school facilities were often sub-standard lacking play areas and specialist rooms. Toby Young led the way with one such school. He was too much of a flamboyant right-wing ideologue to be mainstream in the academy movement. He certainly was a champion of free schools and gained much media attention for his West London Free School in 2011 that he said would be based on 'discipline, ambition and a competitive atmosphere'. The school failed to recruit or fulfil its promise, and in resigning he said he 'regretted his earlier criticism of teachers' and that running schools was more difficult than he had imagined. Association with a person like Young was always fraught with reputational dangers, recalling his earlier statements that 'wheelchair ramps are part of "ghastly" inclusivity in schools', and his improper, jokey comments on the size of women's breasts, which one presumes influenced his resignations from the board of the University Regulator and the Office of Students. It is obviously ground-breaking and innovatory to allow unqualified, forceful people with strongly-held views, like Young, to take the reins of an education establishment and shake it up a bit, after the mediocrity when the Labour government and local authorities were running the show (see chapter 2). Free schools and University Technical Colleges are being absorbed into the MAT structures, so we are rid of these unpredictable and uncontrolled outliers.

There are lessons to be learnt in our changing education landscape from the United States system where Charter schools etc are given many of the 'freedoms' now offered to, or forced on, English schools. The flow is all one way even if conversion numbers to academy status have slowed. Ofsted is helpful in forcing academisation of schools deemed to be 'inadequate' and we can claim that schools in this category stand a greater chance of long-term improvement under academy conditions, even if the statistical evidence suggests otherwise (see subsection *Turning schools around* in Chapter 4). Humbug, of course, and if the fragmentation, or disaggregation as we would rather call it, works in the USA, it will surely work in England

In this free, unsupervised governance environment, some schools designated 'good' or 'outstanding' have head teachers attracted to convert with the promise of increased funding and greater autonomy. While there is a government bribe (meaning 'compensatory incentive') to cover some of the legal costs of conversion, £30,000 at the current time, all state schools are funded at the same per-pupil rate and the only real *financial* gain is for the 'senior' members of the MAT, but strong, entrepreneurial, stable leadership deserves no less. Lucky schools who committed to conversion before 31 March 2015 were offered a bonus £70,000, some even were cold-called by DfE officials to encourage them to convert. In addition, academies could draw on the very substantial Condition Improvement Fund (CIF), to which LA schools do not have access, another treat for the academy sector.

These entrepreneurial skills are important if the freedom to convert is to be maximally exploited in the absence of oversight and regulation. There are several good, commercial tactics that compliant heads can use when trying to win over governing bodies to the academisation cause. It would be simply negligent not to apply them.

1. Convince the governors that local authority funding will be so depleted as to create serious financial difficulties in the near future. Austerity has resulted in school budgets declining and there will need to be 'economies'.
2. Keep the academisation proposal secret as long as possible to prevent a community backlash. (Some heads have suggested that this agenda item is confidential regardless of the terms of governance.)
3. Suggest a false sense of urgency to save the school from a financial meltdown.
4. Wheel in the smooth-talking, suited director of the MAT you might join.
5. Introduce some new governors to the board who will be supportive of the proposal, people bringing 'valuable' experience in areas such as finance and contract law.
6. Convince senior staff who are on the governing board that there will be 'positions' for them if the deal goes through.
7. Assure governors that this change will secure the future of 'our' school, its success and sustainability.

It is difficult for governors to resist a successful head teacher who knows all the buttons to push in these discussions and, of course, if a school fails its Ofsted then these tactics are mainly redundant because the RSC will direct conversion even if there is a local campaign against it.

Fortunately, the justification for breaking-up local authority education departments has taken a hold in parts of the education establishment. An esteemed professor of education at University College London eulogised the transformation of an East End school in London where she had some dealings. She stated that

St Paul's Way School, E3, one of the most deprived postcodes in the country, had been in a poor state before it became a trust and that it was now 'outstanding' and the centre of a MAT. Unfamiliar with the history, she was publicly critical of the work that had gone on in the 4 decades before this. She might not have done all her homework because, a few years before the change, all the staff had been given cash bonuses for being one of the most improved schools in London. This was before the government moved the goalposts and introduced maths and English as part of the benchmark making it difficult for schools like this with 90 per cent EAL pupils. No wonder the school plummeted down the league tables, an experience common across the country with schools in deprived areas. The school also successfully integrated a year 10 cohort of initially not very happy boys from a single sex Hackney school that was closed down. The professor also forgot to mention that, following the award, a period of abysmal leadership ensued with several poor heads and senior leaders employed who largely ignored the stable and dedicated staff who had achieved the award. These senior leaders set in place a 'top-down' regime where experience and local knowledge were ignored. Nor did she mention that the 'improvement' in the school was in the large part a result of a complete new build, always attractive to parents and pupils, and an element of 'social cleansing' that was part of the local regeneration scheme and that many 'difficult' pupils disappeared from the roll. The school is certainly successful by the criteria that count, but staff turnover is massive and the stability and sense of belonging that she stated was the foundation of a good school has been lost. Many of the teachers who had been awarded bonuses were still in the school when it was deemed to be failing – it had had stability – but many of them refused to sign the new contracts and left. There was some grumpiness from those in the know but it has to be accepted that with the ups and downs of a school's history, it is better as an academy if it is caught on a 'down', and that is the end of the story.

Forced academisation: a worked example of how to do it

There are fun and games to be had in being the MAT assigned to take over a school judged inadequate by Ofsted. Admittedly, it is a double-edged sword as such schools require a lot of work but, being in the academy sector, there are all sorts of inducements from the Department for Education and even from recalcitrant LAs to make the takeover easier. Local protests are a further issue but they can be quite fun too when we have the ultimate advantage and they cannot even get the most radical of councils to back them. Big MATs are in charge and the minnows in the field have just not got the credibility, staying power, political nous and sheer 'personality' to get the job done.

An academy order is issued by the Secretary of State for Education and the direction to join a MAT is an instruction with which the LA must comply. Take the case of the London Borough of Greenwich's The John Roan, a school dating back to 1677 when Mr Roan's charity school was set up after a royal bequest and he willed the money for a school for the 'town-born children of Greenwich'. It is situated very close to Greenwich Park on two sites, one old and historic, the other completed in 2014. This one is a real gift for a MAT – nice area, history, ex-grammar, loads of kudos. Turned round it would be attractive to parents and a big feather in the academy chain's cap.

The road to academisation

September 2017 The John Roan School was in trouble with poor results and its third head in 4 years had departed. The LA contracts with the small but local University Schools Trust (UST) which ran two academies – St Paul's Way all-through school in Tower Hamlets and Royal Greenwich Trust School. Support given to John Roan included a new acting head part-time and other staff development and curriculum inputs.

March 2018 Ofsted inspection. Result expected to be RI at best.

June 2018 Publication of Inspection report: 'Inadequate'.

UST named as the DfE's preferred sponsor.

July–December 2018 Challenges made to the conduct and result of the inspection and a call for the academy order to be rescinded, partly on the grounds that the LA was best placed and the democratic organisation to carry through the school improvement.

Protests and action against the takeover by UST by the two unions, GMB over threat to TAs' conditions of service/employment, and NEU over change of employer and lack of consultation and challenge to the Ofsted judgement. A body of parents, John Roan Resists, campaigned, with considerable vigour. LA said to be carrying out 'due diligence', thus slowing the progress towards a conversion date.

December 2018 UST withdrew saying that the school has a 'wide-range of deeply embedded educational, financial and operational challenges that will require a truly exceptional level of investment and a sponsor with extensive resources'. Protesters see it as a vindication of their strategy of digging up every possible piece of dirt on the UST. The 'best' of protesters are merciless and in this case bombarded the UST and other organisations with Freedom of Information (FoI) requests, dug up material on UST CEO Grahame Price's earlier headship at Wilmington Enterprise College in Wilmington which went into special measures soon after his departure and after he had taken 4 months' leave in South America in the run-up to his leaving the school. They had reports of high staff turnover at St Paul's Way Trust School and reports of safeguarding issues stonewalled by the school's management.

January 2019 An Interim Executive Board replaces the governing body.

February–April 2019 United Learning Trust (ULT) and its CEO Jon Coles show 'interest' in taking over the school. ULT had 72 schools, therefore a 'big fish'. Outsiders can only speculate on what happens behind the scenes but it was probably a busy time for ULT: close examination of the school, talks with the DfE about additional funding that might be needed and with the LA about repair bills. One can only speculate that any sensible business would woo the head teacher, make clear the LA's subservient position but that the MAT is there to save their school which is becoming an embarrassment to them and warn them off over-doing the due diligence, a well-known and successful delaying tactic.

March 2019 HMI visitation. Confirmed progress but not enough to be other than 'Inadequate' still.

May 2019 ULT confirmed as the new sponsor.

Change of councillor responsible for Education and Children's Services, possibly a sign that the council leadership had had enough of this shilly-shallying and soft approach to protests and strikes and, if ULT are to be kept on board, they need someone in place sympathetically overseeing on behalf of the borough the progress towards handover, someone more resigned to the legal realities, even if the council had passed a motion months before marking its implacable opposition to academies. The John Roan Resists group continues to be very active with Facebook and Whatsapp groups and well-attended meetings with some big name speakers from union, university and other anti-academy campaigns.

At the same time there is evidence of some parents tiring of the strikes, lost days and general lack of improvement in the school, a wish to see stability and progress. The council is also aware of other schools in the borough complaining that they cannot get advisers in as all the effort is directed towards John Roan. A timely point at which to move strongly and publicly on the takeover of the school.

June 2019 Three big hitters from ULT, seated at the front with the head teacher, present skilfully to 50 parents at a hastily arranged meeting, likely at short-notice to bring in only the committed. The ULT CEO reiterated the Inspectors' monitoring visit findings and projected for all to see the bad data about the school: poor results, poor behaviour, 50 staff on current HR procedures, 40 of which were for absence. Then he outlined what ULT had to offer: staff, ULT curriculum materials, leadership support, behaviour package, all presented politely as a package way beyond what the LA could offer or had offered. Questions largely supportive and negative statements and enquiries handled calmly and confidently.

Council cabinet meeting held to discuss and decide on the steps to getting everything in place for 1 September handover. About 30 protesters, noisily present, outside the town hall and then in the chamber where 'Academisation of the John Roan School' was the first agenda item. After an acknowledgement by the leader of the council that feelings ran high, he asked for calm and respect. The Director of Children's Services began with a determined account of why the academisation had to take place and the six items were all about delegating to various officers the jobs of handling the conversion, finance land and the ever present 'peppercorn rent'. There was some uproar and the meeting was adjourned for calm to settle. Councillors returned. The union representative gave an impassioned speech but there was no budging the council view. There was no discussion. The motion was passed unanimously, though there was no sight of any voting. One assumes there was backroom briefing and the position was made plain that voting against this was voting to break the law.

July–August 2019 ULT increasingly present in the school with new structures designated, Discipline Policy (with **Disruption Free Learning Environment**) and uniform requirements sent to parents.

September 2019. Job done.

What we learn from this is that if the ground is properly prepared by the MAT they will succeed. They have the law behind them and the same government that made the law so swiftly in 2010 has also stripped finance away from the LA so that it is a very weakened force when it comes to school improvement, especially for the challenge of turning around a big secondary. Be ready for the community opposition which will always seem bigger than it is partly because it will be fired up. Answer the questions, be brazen about the high pay and the few mistakes. Deal carefully with the council who after all have little to fight with and, befriended, they will be only too happy to hand the school over. Dazzle all opposition with your mottos and achievements and the good things that you can promise. Do not talk about how many staff will be gone and how ruthless the zero-tolerance behaviour policy will be. That can emerge later and all you have to say is, 'It was worse than we thought.'

Solutions are never simple, as the St Paul's Way and John Roan examples illustrate. The Blob would say that success could be achieved with long-term commitment and by supporting and appreciating the professionalism of teachers and not going for a quick-fix rebranding. They are wrong and these old-fashioned values have lost their appeal.

Regulations slack or entirely absent – can get away with almost anything

Local authority schools have the burden of LA education staff breathing down their necks if they do not follow the laid down procedures. That is no way to efficient operation. Academies are free to operate as they see fit – like rampant buccaneers, some say – in the following areas:

1. Pay and recruitment
2. Staff discipline and dismissal

3. Curriculum content and teaching methods
4. Exclusions – calling them managed moves/transfers but in effect off-rolling
5. Governance and local consultations
6. Estate leasing and ownership
7. Management of special needs
8. Contracting out work and 'related-party transactions'[50].

Academies are not absolutely free in all these areas but appeals and complaints can bob around forever until people give up. That is indeed the biggest weapon when regulation is weak and complainants must climb the ladder to national tribunal and judicial review levels. Once it gets to that level, the academy can make some conciliatory noises, possibly even suffer a small compensation payment in the case of an Ombudsman ruling, but the problem goes away cheaply.

Pay and recruitment

We have given instances of the well-deserved pay packets chief execs can earn (see table in Chapter 7). Some people, right up to Lord Agnew, Parliamentary Under-Secretary of State for the School System, happily report that the school resource management advisers (RMAs) – normally school business managers – found £35 million of 'essentially misdirected resources' at 72 schools and trusts, which amounted to a 'colossal sum of money'[51] (the report was later withdrawn, including from the internet). Making those savings is not so difficult for the business brain. One piece of advice is to replace experienced teachers with support staff on term-time-only contracts. Another, to combat the large expenditure on supply cover, was to adopt an 'alternative model (i.e. using existing spare staff capacity to cover three classes at a time in the dining hall) thus saving nearly £50,000', the equivalent of one full-time upper pay teacher. There are suggestions for the reduction of the numbers of subjects at

Key Stage 5, A-Levels and a review of the length of the school week. There were also the smaller portions for school dinners.

The most powerful implicit messages are not to recruit or retain staff who are some way up the pay scale, be really harsh with targets and associated performance-related pay and clamp down on sickness. This is the way to run an education business, more like a laundrette or widget production factory than we used to think.

Staff discipline and dismissal

It is well known that getting rid of a weak member of staff or someone who is off sick too often can be problematic. We have always known how to make people's lives unbearable so they leave but, free from LA oversight and governors totally on our side, we can take this harassment to a new level.

Warwick Mansell gives an example, not naming the academy or the MAT but the process is the usual. Union's divisional secretary submits a complaint to the Department for Education, expressing worry:

about the behaviour of an academy chain's management. As a caseworker for the NUT, I have experienced occasions (this year) in this same school of bullying NUT members. On the most recent occasion it has involved a member who has been diagnosed with 'severe anxiety'. This teacher had made a 'protected disclosure' admitting to his depression, but had then been bullied...Instead of being supported, he has come under attack twice and been put on two separate disciplinary charges and had his capability called into question. In addition, [staff at the chain have] ignored the Occupational Health report where advice was given about how to manage his health condition.

Mansell went on to describe the chain of exchanges. A response from the ESFA said the issues raised were outside its remit. It pointed to the government's official complaints procedure for academies, adding that, 'You will see from this that the issues you raise regarding your client's employment at…Academy Trust do not fall into any of the areas the ESFA can investigate. The issues are more appropriate to be raised through the academy's and trust's own grievance procedures or taken to an employment tribunal.'

Checking the document, to which the ESFA referred, he found that it does indeed say that complaints by parents [or anyone else, one imagines] have to be considered by the academy itself in the first place, following a set of rules laid down in this document. Only then will the ESFA investigate, and only then in terms of whether it has complied with: a) its own complaints procedure; b) the terms of its funding agreement with the Secretary of State; c) with its legal obligations[52]. This is as wonderfully weak as Michael Gove and the academy sector as a whole would want it to be, putting the academy or MAT in the position of investigating itself.

A second example refers to 'a tirade to staff' at Birchen Coppice Primary Academy in Kidderminster. Andrew Morrish, the chief executive of the Victoria Academies Trust (VAT) and former Ofsted Inspector, threatened to uncover and 'deal with' the anonymous whistleblower who had behaved in a 'treacherous', 'underhand' and 'pathetic' way[53]. An employee wrote to Ofsted raising issues relating to safeguarding, trust expenditure and treatment of staff. The CEO, with the sort of forthrightness the state school sector may too slowly be coming to terms with, is quoted as saying: 'Even though it's got "anonymous", I am determined to find out who is behind it. And whoever is behind it, I'll deal with.'

It would be no surprise to learn that *Protect*, the whistleblowing charity, considered this 'disgraceful'. There may well be statutory duties not to subject people 'to detriment' for making public interest disclosures but, whether or not these so-called disclosures are mischievous, the sort of response made by Mr Morrish is quite understandable in this new era.

Curriculum content and teaching methods

Teach what you like, but academies will be subject to the same metrics as other schools. The business case for restricting the curriculum is obvious so that one never has ridiculously small classes for some subjects 'because five pupils opted for sociology GCSE' or some other 'pupil negotiation' or wrong-headed 'customer choice' reason. An academy might well have a range of extra-curricular activities, and these are very good for public presentation of the school, local press stories and strong selling/recruitment points, so are worth doing for those reasons alone. There is the suggestion that a formal curriculum defined by a MAT for its academies could be restricted, 'so potentially reducing educational opportunities for the pupils who attend them'[54]. Academies have no need to worry as there are few parent or education experts who complain credibly.

Exclusions: managed moves/transfers, off-rolling

There is statutory guidance governing exclusions and the latest is the DfE 2017 *Exclusion from maintained schools, academies and pupil referral units*. If you want to Off-roll, you should look carefully at the *Education Act 2006* on admissions and how a pupil may be removed from the school roll. The local authority school head teachers who play fast and loose with the procedures for moving a child on would be corrected by the local authority. The LA has no such direct role with academies, though they can try. An academy might be caught out by Ofsted and it could result in a bad inspection report, to which discovered off-rolling could contribute, and this could lead to funding being axed and assignment to a new trust, a threat issued to Shenley Academy in Birmingham. The MAT implicated was E-Act, which insisted it was conducting a 'thorough investigation' into the inspectorate's findings that eight year 11 pupils were removed on the same day shortly before the school census. The Ofsted report said leaders, 'could not give any valid explanation as to why eight pupils, all of whom were disadvantaged and half had SEND, were removed from the school's roll on the same day in the autumn term 2017....This practice suggests off-rolling[55].' The message is there: be careful and while you can stretch the rules, don't break them.

In relation to data on suspected off-rolling and the robustness of response, the IDSR (inspection data summary report) noted exceptional levels of *pupil movement* between years 10 and 11, i.e. pupils coming off the roll of a school, accepting that there are entirely legitimate reasons a pupil may move off a school roll lawfully, but 'if inspectors have concerns about potential "off-rolling", they must discuss them with the school leaders during the inspection'. Not so tough.

The Ofsted Blog reports that, 'Academies, particularly those in some multi-academy trusts, appear to be losing proportionately more pupils than local authority schools. Conversely, local authority schools seem to be taking on proportionately more pupils.' There have been many examples of MATs off-rolling pupils with special needs in pursuit of improvements in national tests and examinations.

Academies, supported by their MATs, can use exclusions to get rid of pupils, or pressure parents to take the pupil away or face exclusions, all in the cause of enforcing the behaviour policy and creating a pupil population committed to learning, committed to those key words in an academy's motto. It has to be done, however, with charm ('I'm sorry, but there is no other way') and subtlety ('Are you sure he/she would not be happier at another school?).

Thankfully and sensibly, appeals procedures in the far less regulated world of academies and MATs mean compliance and enforcement are weak. Take the case of M, a special needs pupil at Ark Greenwich Free School (AGFS) who was permanently excluded, but the parent when called to a meeting with the head was gently pressed to sign a permanent exclusion waiver 'so that it would not be on M's record forever'. The case would go to the Fair Access Panel (FAP) for an offer of a new school. The failure of the school to send in the necessary documentation, including a form signed by the parent meant that it did not go to FAP, the school lost patience and M was assigned to a local Alternative Provision (AP) and the file sent there. The academy, quite reasonably, called it a *managed transfer*. The parent at this point was angry at how the child had been dumped and wanted to appeal to the school governors as the exclusion or transfer had not been properly carried out.

Complaints went in to Ofsted (who, it is believed, did send a note to the LA) but the response was 'not one for us'. The DfE referred the complaint to the EFSA who said it should go to the school and to the MAT head office. This was sent to info@arkonline.org and 1 month later there had been no response. The local authority had the borough's solicitor send in one of those sharp letters that only a legal office can to the head teacher referring to two acts of parliament and two sets of associated statutory regulations, demanding, yes demanding, a reply within 7 days. Nothing was sent back with any urgency and when the reply from the school did arrive, it cleverly disregarded the demands for clear explanation and conveyed a 'Can't we just move on?' message. Similarly, the CEO of the Trust when alerted to the dispute responded calmly, 'I can reassure you that I am confident that AGFS have fulfilled their statutory duties. The school takes its responsibility to vulnerable students very seriously, they work effectively with the Local Authority, and operate actively within the agreed Fair Access protocols.' Job done. Brush off nearly complete. The parent is tempted to put the whole business aside and wait for a mainstream school for the child. There is always the possibility of a complaint to the ESFA about the school and to the Local Authority Ombudsman about the LA's failure to enforce the requirement for the school to go through FAP for an exclusion or managed move, but sanctions resulting would be inconsequential and the effort required considerable.

Had this been an LA school it would have been for LA officers to enforce the regulations. Academy-world in England is different and these are the steps, the blank walls and silences, to thwart an appeal/complaint. It is amusing to witness, and if the parent, local authority, or 'concerned citizen' wanted to take up the 'illegality', bear in mind that academy chains have better lawyers for sure.

Governance and local consultations

Academies do not have to have local representation, either from the local authority, its councillors or parents. They can also change their Planned Admission Numbers (PAN) without consultation because they are defined as being their own admissions authority, which can complicate local planning for school places which does rest with the LA

Academies recruit children mostly from the local area, the local authority in which they are situated. Having left the local authority to become an academy, whether voluntarily or forced, there is a severe break with local control and only in regard to admissions, special needs and child protection does the LA have a role. In some cases, academies do cooperate with the Fair Access Panel and take pupils assigned to them. More often, the academy cooperates grudgingly in such arrangements and a number have been known to opt out when it does not suit them and when they think they can avoid taking a pupil who will not 'be a credit' to them. This is an arrangement absolutely in keeping with the independence of an academy or MAT.

Some schools will go slightly over number when a new arrival applies but often any school, especially a 'free' academy, will not allow the admission of a pupil unlikely to do well and suggest to the parent of a pupil with special needs, EAL or who obviously brings problems that 'the school down the road' does really well with your sort of child. Halley House Free School in Hackney, part of the Bellevue Place Education Trust, has been unusually explicit in manoeuvring in such a way that it would not have to take onto their roll a large number of special needs and English as a second language children. The head said it was to protect the school's existing children and 'provide the highest quality education provision to the children who had joined and not be compromised by the addition of one or two pupils during the year'[56]. So he lowered the PAN (Planned Admissions Number). That stopped newcomers and the results improved. That is the way to do it.

Estate leasing and ownership

In the area of land and plant, the academy sector is especially favoured. The government is so keen to privatise education, a school site is virtually given away. Here's the deal; we get the buildings for nothing – a peppercorn rent on a 125-year lease – and here is the best bit: the local authorities and the taxpayers have to pay for repairs before we take over the leases and they give us the money for the legal fees to complete the transaction. What's not to like? If anyone raises objections about giving away their heritage, friends in government and the media will insist that this is progress. As well as the buildings, we get access to the whole shebang – staff, curriculum, supply chain, even the necessary raw material – the pupils. A goldmine.

Academies and free schools have the benefit of association with the property company called LocatED, operated 'at arms length' it will find new properties for free schools for which it has been allocated £2bn. This is huge generosity for the privatised sector and it is unfortunate that they have screwed up – or perhaps it was just one of those bad ideas: £33M for a secondary free school in north London next to two existing schools, cancelling a project in Hertfordshire after £19M expenditure[57].

Warning: be careful and do not be too obviously greedy and learn the lesson of what happened to the following:

Sir Greg Martin, knighted for services to education at Gove's suggestion, awarded a £400,000 salary – nought wrong with that – but he had a financial interest in a dating agency[58] run from the school site as well as the gym and swimming pool. That is taking things too far even by our purposely relaxed standards.

The Conservative Party donor and Parliamentary Under-secretary for Schools with responsibility for academies, free schools and the Education Funding Agency, Lord John Nash, is also pushing the boundaries. He is co-founder and partner in Sovereign Capital, a private equity company that specialises in the provision of support services to health and education, so what insider trading opportunities were coming his way. Surely not from Future Academies MAT (libertas per cultum: Latin always gives gravitas) and its six schools with himself and wife as trustees and directors[59].

If the academy sector is restrained all will be well. You have the Conservative Party behind you. In 2012, the Conservative think tank the Institute of Economic Affairs published *The Profit Motive in Education: Continuing the Revolution*, arguing that 'The Conservative reforms to education would not be complete until for-profit companies had been wholeheartedly welcomed into schools.' These reforms include the production and sale of schemes of work and how to teach them as well as servicing the fabric of the buildings etc. 'Academies and free schools should become profit-making businesses using hedge funds and venture capitalists to raise money,' according to private plans drawn up by Michael Gove as Education Secretary. Mosaica, the Curriculum Centre, Kidzania[60] and many others are waiting to pounce. The message is: 'Get some of the action while the going is good.'

Management of special needs

On special needs, you have to talk the talk but children with learning or behavioural issues are not the best material to work with. Everyone knows that.

Across the country, in 2019, there were protests about not enough places for SEND pupils, insufficient support when they are in schools, long delays in assessments and the completion and implementation of Education and Health Care Plans (EHCP). Academies have no special responsibility here but one of the cost-cutting strategies is to reduce the number of Teaching Assistants (TAs), and academies are said to stand out. Halley Academy ('Shaping lives, transforming communities') in south London, part of the Leigh Academy Trust (LAT) seeking to make 19 TAs redundant to avoid a deficit. Sixteen of the staff have been made redundant with the GMB union representative complaining, 'many of our members look after the most vulnerable children in the school and yet LAT were suggesting they should leave this Friday and not come back with no clear plan in place to support the children who rely on this vital service'.[61] Academies have to hold firm with their financial imperatives, even if thousands are protesting at the lack of SEND funding and handing in a petition to Downing Street (30 May 2019).

A recent study[62] found that 26 per cent of children with Education and Health Care Plans (EHCP) or disability (SEND) do not go on to reception classes in the school where they went to preschool, contrasting with only 18 per cent of children with no recorded SEND. There is the suggestion that schools are avoiding admitting SEND pupils who may adversely affect their results. They hypothesise that funding cuts and target-based school accountability measures disincentivise schools from admitting these pupils, and local authorities have reduced capacity to address inequalities in early-years provision. They report that there is also evidence that some schools discourage (more or less explicitly) admission to reception classes of children with complex needs. Academies, naturally, get more than their fair share of the blame for this, regardless of any evidence beyond anecdotes

Academies can withstand the charges that they are especially guilty of resisting admissions of SEND children. Berkeley Primary School in Gloucestershire, part of the Cotswold Beacon Academy Trust, could not offer the support the hospital consultant recommended for a child, but the trust said, without irony, 'Berkeley is a highly successful school which provides a caring and stimulating learning environment for all children in its care and that at all times has qualified personnel to ensure that children are safe and looked after[63].' This is happening everywhere. The response is to claim the high ground, whether you are on it or not.

Who needs regulation, procedures and enforcement?

The simple answer is, 'Not us!' The academy sector thrives in an environment characterised by freedom and reward for entrepreneurial effort and effect. We have a responsibility to show how we can take advantage of this, especially as our allies have impoverished the resources of any competition. Central government has taken money from LAs, so what is the point of any school, 'outstanding', 'good' or otherwise staying within that fold? The additional grants for buildings, the services we can contract ourselves from wherever, the control or entry and exit of pupils to our academies and even 'adjusting' a school's deficit before takeover are such advantageous conditions, we cannot fail. Taking over a failing school in the face of virulent opposition from parents is no great strain for a competent MAT. A MAT can offer a small team to improve subject management, behaviour policies and practice, bespoke curriculum materials, coaching of key staff, elimination of unwanted staff and the LA, by contrast, can offer very, very little. The market is rigged in our favour and we must go forth and multiply, brushing off the criticisms and championing our brand.

10. Forget democracy and local responsibility for schools

Introduction

Of course, you don't want to *forget* democracy in the running of local schools; you want to **wipe it out**. If you've done the job well up to now, you have screwed them locally, side-lined local councillors, got solid links with government ministers and officials and reduced surveillance and regulatory control. Now you can get on with the important business of paying yourselves bumper salaries, sub-contracting to the in-laws and trusted mates, and grinding teachers and children into the ground.

Who needs democracy when it comes to education? What use were local councillors or advisers in managing schools? Were governing bodies ever any good at 'governing'?

Now we have a business model, not some limp social service model all about care and pastoral stuff while pupils 'grow'. We are not into mental bloody health or fun and joy. Just get the buggers to behave[64] and watch the scores on the doors; it is all about the results, exam and test results, and 'all the rest is noise'[65].

Democratic deficit

When Tony Blair's government introduced the concept of academies in 2002, they were justified on the grounds that only so-called *persistently failing schools* would be taken out of local authority control and supported by sponsors who would commit fairly large sums of money and 'drag' these difficult institutions up to an acceptable standard. This process involved the establishment of a board of trustees in each new academy and very limited local authority involvement – often much to their relief. A number of high-profile individuals and organisations came on board and whether this was entirely because they had a deep commitment to education and genuine philanthropic intentions or whether part of their motivation was to curry favour with the Blair government or make money is debatable. At that time, it was the palest of third way actions. By the end of the Labour government in 2010 there were 203 academies in 83 local authorities. In 2019, after the swiftly introduced Academies Act of 2010 supercharged and transformed the third way into a privatised takeover, there are over 8000 with all barriers gloriously and profitably swept away and an annual cache worth over £20 billion available and growing.

The result was a series of schools operating independently of their communities. In some cases there was a notable improvement in examination grades but often this was not sustained over the years. Some trustees' visions of education were built on their experiences of quite formal grammar or private schools where school uniform and discipline became the priorities rather than a soft-centred curriculum offering all things and centring on pupil engagement. Under this system schools were able to offer higher salaries to head teachers and senior leaders through the sponsors' financial contributions and slowly the profession became more attractive to financially motivated staff who were prepared to undermine the ridiculous, myopic principle that teaching was primarily a caring profession and not a winner-grabs-all business.

Gradually, stand-alone academies were taken over by academy chains, MATs. Many MATs expanded geographically to achieve national coverage, with schools separated by great distances, quite unlike the LAs. ULT has schools from Cumbria to Kent.

This move away from local democracy was very appealing to a Tory party which saw in it the long-term possibility of full privatisation and so built the expansion of academies into their 2010 manifesto and have, since the coalition government of that year, made it increasingly difficult or unattractive for schools to remain within their local authority. Financial inducements were offered for a quick transfer to a MAT and the law was changed by the Education and Adoption Act of 2016 to force a school to transfer if it failed its Ofsted inspection. There is much evidence to suggest helpful complicity in this from Ofsted. To further break-up the local authorities, the coalition and subsequent Tory governments have encouraged the establishments of free schools where a group of parents or an interested organisation can seek funding to establish their own school, and local authorities have to aid this process even if, as is often the case, the proposal is for a site where there is no shortage of places locally. This is at the outer edge of 'freedom' and some of these free schools have failed or been taken over by academy chains, thus sorting out this aberration.

This diversity has many advantages for the Tory party and business associates:

1. creates an extensive market where there was a very limited one;
2. paves the way for ultimate privatisation;
3. allows the government to have even more control of the curriculum;
4. introduces greater competition between schools and local authorities and between MATs and free schools;
5. undermines further what is left of national pay and conditions agreements as MATs and free schools do not have to employ qualified teachers, although most do;
6. makes it increasingly difficult for trade unions to operate within the education sector as academies do not have to recognise unions or provide facilities time;
7. reduces the dissatisfaction with central government's financial settlements on education by directing some of the criticism at boards of trusts etc;
8. allows much more freedom for private contractors to

operate ancillary services and with so many boards of trustees it makes scrutiny of these contracts and their awarding processes increasingly difficult. (There have been many examples of MATs etc awarding contracts without suitable tendering processes and some dubious awards going to family or friends);

9. creates in schools a sense of fear both for teachers and other staff where the managers feel able to threaten and bully and massively increase workloads with little opportunity for staff to complain. If they do complain, the threat of 'capabilities procedures' is quickly raised and staff are 'encouraged' to resign and move on.

What's not to like?

The bigger picture

The academy movement is but one part of larger national and international developments where big money presses for more relaxed control of facilities, services and enterprises once run by the state. The strong message that 'state works poorly, private works well' reverberates across the world and some write of GERM (global education reform movement). These international developments draw sustenance from OECD international performance indicators and proceed on an upward trajectory without evidence of improved standards and even in spite of a stream of reports on vested interests benefitting, surreptitious profit-making, fraud, 'managing' pupil intake to advantage, falsifying attainment data and removing staff. Amazingly, the privatisation machine can churn out the good news, grab the publicity and drown out the more worrying developments. The state relinquishing of control and responsibility for this key national institution has led to casualties but these have to be for the national good: child poverty has increased; social mobility has stalled; the economy is not working; foodbanks have increased four-fold in 10 years; parents are campaigning about inadequate provision for special needs. The Local Government Association (LGA) reveals that, overall, councils will have suffered a 77 per cent decrease in government funding between 2015/16 and 2020, from £9927M to £2284M. This has little or nothing to do with neo-liberal, privatising agendas and we need to keep hammering this home

According to data from the Department for Education, budgets for early intervention children's services, designed to stop family problems such as abuse and neglect spiralling out of control, have dropped by £743M in the last 5 years. Over the same period, government spending on Sure Start, children's centres and other universal family services has dropped by £450M – a decrease of 42 per cent. There are more children in care, there is a surge in child protection cases. And then we have Philip Alston, United Nations rapporteur, following a 2-week flit around Britain in November 2018, reporting on poverty, inequality and all the bad things he could find quoted as saying, 'You are really screwing yourselves royally for the future by producing a sub-standard workforce and children that are malnourished.' This is impolite and unhelpful, if true. Modern neo-liberalism creates a few winners and lots of losers, but that is only in the short-term. Austerity has to be dealt with and a country cannot simply tax its way out of trouble even if little Finland does.

England's education 2019

Once there might have been genuine praise and pride for an educational environment where pupils feel safe and know that there is a good prospect that many teachers will be around for their whole time in the school. Trust and reliability were thought important factors in the 'growing process'. Education was not only about the imparting of information that could be regurgitated at test time; it was about personal development and the building of relationships with both other pupils and the staff.

There are examples of today's MATs doing the most wonderful and strange things: imposing a strict silence regime in corridors between lessons; this is Albany School in Hornchurch, Essex[66]. Ninestiles in Birmingham is said to be trying the same with detention if caught speaking between classes. Ranking all the pupils in a year group from top to bottom and making sure they and their parents know where they stand; that was Burlington Danes School back in 2015 under the now Dame Sally Coates (currently ULT), bringing a military style discipline into schools and 'flattening the grass' at Outwood Grange Academy Trust. It is all worth a try, when there has been comprehensive rubbishing of education as it was and of the organisations running it. These professionals know what they are doing. They are good people.

It is not all unalloyed success, however. There is resistance, and in recent years many establishments have fought off the threat of academisation with unbelievable viciousness. This has usually been achieved by galvanising parents and staff around the banner of, 'This school belongs to us, the local community.' With that unjustified faith in local councils and their elected representatives whom they want to oversee the efficient running of our local authority, they do not want hard-earned assets given away to a board that has little accountability and, in most cases, excludes elected parents from the school's governing body and certainly from the MAT's trustee board. But this is unfair, below the belt stuff when they dig up stories on the trust CEO from 8 years back, send in an unending stream of Freedom of Information requests, scrutinise the MAT and individual academy accounts at Companies House, and put out scurrilous stories about backroom deals and that the lead inspector knows someone in the MAT later designated to take over a failing school.

Those campaigns have involved parents, trade unions and schools' wider communities. Trade unions carry a lot of weight in these situations and, unfortunately, most teachers and ancillary staff are still members, but their difficulty is in persuading staff to be actively involved all the time and not just when a crises occurs. It is also increasingly difficult to get volunteers to take on the role of union representative because with ever-increasing school meetings and exam/test pressure, staff feel worn-down but there is always the threat of 'capability' we can use for a representative who does the job (too) well. Governors are vital to have onside if the head is trying to convert to academy status, because often they will try to impose a sense of urgency on the discussions insisting sometimes that discussions around the issue are kept 'confidential', a useful, if outrageous, tactic that can work to cut down time available for protest when the plan becomes public. Local authority governors might feel it is their job to 'blow the whistle' if there is the mention of academisation, so hoodwink them, buy them off or compromise them early on. Stories abound about MAT boards having agenda items hidden without the local community of the schools in the MAT being represented.

The Blob is not greatly to be feared when they call it all a mess, chaos, unscrupulous, bullying, exploitative and then, in that child-like way of theirs, suggest that the way forward out of this is for a new system to be developed by opposition parties, who oppose creeping (or is it racing?) privatisation of education. In their slow, rambling discussions over years, they see promise of dramatic change to the landscape when a less authoritarian and more liberal and socially minded government comes to power. One ludicrous idea being developed by Labour in opposition is a National Education Service that would find a way to return 'our' education system to one that really is outstanding and, 'blue-sky-thinking', makes the private sector feel challenged in its assumption of superiority. A start would be a reversal of austerity and provision of funding for state schools that enables better facilities, smaller classes and more support. This is so out of touch with the inexorable march of progress led by the entrepreneurial elite. So, there is little to worry about.

The weakness of opposition to the academisation cause is so clearly manifest in the lack of regulation, oversight and enforcement. For high salaries to senior executives the government's Public Accounts Committee refers MATs to guidance in the *Academies Financial Handbook* where it is stated that trustees 'must ensure that their decisions about levels of executive pay follow a robust evidence-based process and are reflective of the individual's role and responsibilities'. Publicly-funded institutions, MATs are reminded, are bound by the Nolan principles of public life, which should give pause for thought when making decisions and trustees need to be especially mindful that public service 'doesn't come with a golden salary goose'. None of this documentation lays out how it must be done or sets limits or imposes external review. So it's over to you, trustees. Make it up as you go along. There really is a bonanza for those who deserve it.

Take care, learn the language and cover your tracks
Now for a warning. Get your narrative right and it should contain the words 'caring', 'nurturing', 'growth' and 'differentiation' (whatever that is). Oh, and 'diversity' with 'multiculturalism', they are good ones. Get a good, smart, public face as though you were really, really interested in 'the children'. Try to say and write that without it sounding cringe-worthy.

Look at the United Learning Trust (ULT) website. This is the largest MAT in terms of number of schools and students. John Smeaton Academy, Leeds states: 'Our mantra is "The Best in Everyone", which is underpinned by our core values of ambition, confidence, creativity, respect, enthusiasm and determination.' This academy has a Behaviour Policy which runs to 31 pages (updated March 2019). Most academies and their MATs are embedded in the corporate world and advertising your wares is second nature.

DO NOT, we repeat, **DO NOT** admit to refusing admission to special needs kids – in fact, big up your SEND department. **DENY** that you off-roll pupils. Say clearly that you did not strongly encourage any parent to home educate, you did not have that conversation with parent or carer about how any more fixed-term exclusions would lead to harsher sanctions and 'wouldn't it be better for both of us if you took him/her away?' State your case for the part-time arrangements you have for some students and, as for the large numbers in your [behaviour] unit with teaching assistants 'containing' challenging students, get really, genuinely loud about how it is restorative even therapeutic in intent, not really about punishment.

Staffing: no, you have not cut staffing to the bone, reduced numbers of teaching assistants and got drama teachers teaching history or cookery.

You have signed up to the purple book plus (National Staff Conditions) and you expect staff to believe that. Sometimes you have to move staff on. Like Nike says, just do it! Do it as near the end of term as you can if you want to limit the time for organised protest; you know how those unions react.

Parents and community: concoct some sort of carefully chosen parent group and you have another line of defence; let them tell your lies – sorry, we mean tell your story.

Services to out-source: there is nothing wrong with paying friends and relations. But do not shout about it. Be out of meetings where the decision is made but of course you have it stitched up beforehand. No conflict of interest there, then. Related-party deals have got a bit of a bad press[67] so do a cover-up job. If anything comes out via an uppity parent, you know the drill: deny, deny, deny. It will go away. Who will believe *them*? You're just doing your job. You're a professional, oh yes.

Uniform and discipline: do not be afraid of the d-word and it does not hurt to tie it in with uniform, right down to socks and type of shoes. It is even possible to get a rake-off by specifying that the business goes via one local clothes store.

Having a relationship with the local authority: don't knock it. Local authorities are a source of dosh even if it is a diminishing stash. You can use the, 'we are educating your children' line and claim they never tended to the upkeep of the school fabric before it became an academy. If you as a Multi-Academy Trust are taking over a school, one that wants to join, a forced academisation or a re-brokering, see what you can squeeze out of the LA, cash-strapped though they might be. This is a trick no business should overlook. You can also try to get a little out of the Regional Schools Commissioner or the ESFA.

Keep an eye on the counter-narrative

There is vocal opposition out there and it would like to think it is a danger. It is not if we keep our guard up and control the agenda. THEY know what they are against but have scarcely a constructive idea between them. The protest groups are wild, and can whip up anti-academy support. The insults can be vile and the personal background material they dig up about career faux pas from way back would be funny if it were not also a little hurtful. Some set up websites and talk about how a trust's 'gorging on vulnerable schools is rapacious' and how it is 'washing hands of pupils with SEN' [how dare they?] Go to a Reclaiming Education gathering in a parliamentary committee room, not a big attendance even with David Wolfe, radical barrister, holding forth about overturning contracts and undermining all that academies have achieved. A room full of old people, almost exclusively white, so rather compromised claims to inclusivity. Then we have the university blob hacks who should have been put out to grass long since, turning out titles like *Miseducation: Inequality, Education and the Working Classes* (Diane Reay, 2017. Policy Press), *Key Issues in Education and Social Justice* (Emma Smith, 2018. Sage), *The Working Class: Poverty, Education and Alternative Voices* (Ian Gilbert, 2018.

Independent Thinking Press), *Knowledge, Policy and Practice: the Struggle for Social Justice in Education* (Andrew Brown and Emma Wisby, 2019.UCL IOE Press). There is the even more ludicrous stuff on neo-liberalism, marketisation, etc as though these people do not know the world has changed and **there is no going back!**

Reviewing where we are

The dismantling challenge is well advanced but will only be sustained and progress further if the steps are regularly revisited. An understanding of and a commitment to a big business, privatising, neo-liberal outlook is the bedrock and must be conveyed as the only option. Rubbish state schools as they are, but patronisingly ('they are doing what they can, poor things'). Get government to cut funding to local authorities and spread the word about how they have failed and would again, given the chance. It is all about standards and that means what we can measure and salaries to the top people will go up even if allocation and attention to the poor and needy goes down. Outsource to your hearts content and maintain the near-invisibility of oversight, direction, control or enforcement. Democracy had its day and still has its place but not at the local level and not running schools.

We are near the nirvana of privatised education, partners in a root and branch takeover of a multi-billion pound service which the government could not, and cannot, run efficiently. A couple of moves would round it off nicely. Collectively, you could pull it off. Here are the tips:

1. Take over Ofsted. Yes, it is possible but not really for us to go into now as it might not be strictly legal.
2. Get some restriction of FoI (Freedom of Information) requests. Stop nosey parkers probing salary levels, your policies (exclusion numbers etc) and your sub-contracting.

3. Train your own staff and, while teachers should have degrees, there is no need for theory and knowledge of child development and stuff like that; engage with Teach First and the Teacher Apprenticeship scheme.

4. This is a global financial world and take care where you place your hard-earned salary plus bonus plus payoff if you do screw up at some point.

5. Plan your future on the board of some MAT, in Ofsted or set up your own consultancy giving a school what it wants. And remember: the more they pay, the more they will value your advice.

Some further tips that might be considered a bit dodgy:

6. Manage your intake to take few, if any, of the following – social housing children, SEND children, free school meals (pupil premium) pupils, looked after children and EALs (English as an Additional Language) and even an excess of boys.

7. Directives from Fair Access Panels (FAPs) and other ways of moving around challenging or disruptive students, don't let them in.

8. In your justifiable attempts to improve the quality of your pupil body, move on the 'undesirables', but not by exclusions. Have that little chat with the parents which suggests, basically, that if they don't take him/her away, you will have to permanently exclude – 'black mark on their record for life'; elective home education might appeal to them.

9. Choose your staff wisely and have a clear-out periodically of those not toeing the line. As well as removing trouble, it is a message to those who remain.

10. Money. You are worth it. Get yourself into the £150K wage bracket as an academy head or the chief executive of a

multi-academy Trust and ensure your senior colleagues are similarly well rewarded. Remember, you could not have done it alone and you may need cover or silence from these colleagues in the future.

You have done it. The ruthless profiteer, that is you. And why not?

Postscript

What happens when a new government comes to power and how to protect academies and associated non-state services. Let's future-proof.

This is to all you crazy edu-preneurs out there who have made it. You run an academy or an academy chain and you are making a fortune out of services you supply to our semi-privatised school sector.

Think what *they* will do to bring you down, install an alternative system or, god forbid, send schools back to local authority control. The Labour Party's National Policy Forum on Local Accountability in the *National Education Service* says the intention is, 'to end the academies and free schools programme and bring all publicly funded schools back into the mainstream public sector ensuring they are democratically accountable to the communities that they serve'. So be warned.

Their biggest weapon is control of law-making. Retrospective law-making is difficult in that it undermines business systems, so get ready to *complain* when the unpicking begins.

Resist by ensuring that land leases of 125 years keep you in control. Get a few PFIs with 30-year maintenance agreements that cannot be bought out.

Their next biggest weapon is finance, and if they are clever they will think like Putin, not the Putin of Novichok etc but the Putin of retrieving BP's oil business from a multinational in such a way that they were, in the end, willing to give him everything and could not get out fast enough.

Resist by tying up the finances in long-term, big-time initiatives, so complex that legal entanglement will put government off punitive measures, especially if parents get up in arms about their children's education being damaged.

Their next biggest weapon is the workforce, which, if it is on your side, can campaign, and even strike, to maintain the system you have fought to establish. If not, then they will collude in taking it right back into the public sector.

Resist by doing pre-emptive cuddling up to the unions nationally and demonstrating to select members of local workforces the benefits (only finance really counts) accruing to them from academised arrangements.

Their fourth biggest weapon is media and the 'selling' of their new (probably old) vision for education and they will hope they get a groundswell of approval from all those lefties, hippies, intellectuals and luvvies who want a soft and easy education experience for their children that gives lots of enjoyment and minimal stress, like the Finns, and views teachers as genuine professionals whose opinions are valued and who are not there to be ignored and abused.

Resist by burnishing your image, manipulate the stats, glorify the best achievements, ride out the scandals because you will never hide them all, and have the best people up-front in any televised, tweeted, blogged presentations/confrontations.

You will not be alone in this fight as the mass of privatised and outsourced enterprises are in the same boat. This is globalised capital, operating with a reinterpretation and new understanding of the '*third* way', achieving a benevolent and effective takeover by entrepreneurs in education, health, prison and probation, transport and power. You are a powerful bloc together.

None of their weapons after that are big. So that is it: laws, finance, the workers and the media. Manage all that and you can carry on as before. Failing that, you could make the schools the best they can be, make the students the happiest in the world, make the teachers the most contented professionals in the land, listen to your local stakeholders, especially parents, and hope you deserve to survive. Please note that you have a long way to go down that track.

You can prosper; you know you can.

Endnotes

1   Spoken by Regan on 12 August, 1986 while president.
2   The key document was published in 2011 https://www.
    networks.nhs.uk/nhs-networks/ahp-networks/documents/
    AQP%20guidance.pdf/view
3   The government's Public Accounts Committee was critical
    of PFIs with criticisms of the Treasury with 'apparently
    institutionalized fuzzy thinking over such large sums
    of public money'. https://www.parliament.uk/business/
    committees/committees-a-z/commons-select/public-
    accounts-committee/news-parliament-2017/private-
    finance-initiatives-report-published-17-19/
4   Private Finance Initiatives began in 1992 under John Major
    and were taken up with enthusiasm by the Blair government
    because you could get big infrastructure projects going,
    without raising taxes and losing popularity, a true third
    way characteristic. http://www.corporate-welfare-watch.
    org.uk/wp/2018/02/19/pfi-schools/
5   Discussion of PFIs, Independent, 25 Sept, 2017. https://www.
    independent.co.uk/news/business/analysis-and-features/
    labour-pfi-john-mcdonnell-scheme-government-hospitals-
    private-finance-initiative-party-conference-a7966521.html
6   UK Public Spending (2019) https://www.ukpublicspending.
    co.uk/year_spending_2020UKbn_17bc9n_20#ukgs302
7   The Education Endowment Foundation's Challenge the Gap
    (CtG) is a 'school to school improvement programme that
    aims to break the link between disadvantage and attainment
    through collaboration and the sharing of best practice
    between schools'. https://educationendowmentfoundation.
    org.uk/projects-and-evaluation/projects/challenge-the-gap/
8   https://www.compare-school-performance.service.gov.uk/
    schools-by-type?hasperfdata=true%2ctrue&hasperfdata=tr

ue&step=default&table=mats&for=secondary&page=1

9   The Learning and Skills Act, 2000, Section 130, Subsection 5 (3B) required the Sec. of State to consult the local authorities. http://www.legislation.gov.uk/ukpga/2000/21/pdfs/ukpga_20000021_en.pdf

10   Jess Staufenberg, 'Named: The 92 academy trusts with multiple staff on £100k+' *Schools Week,* 30 April 2018. https://schoolsweek.co.uk/named-the-92-academy-trusts-with-multiple-staff-on-100k/

11   Guardian 25 Mar 2014. United Learning academy chain accuses DfE of 'acting illegally. https://www.theguardian.com/education/2014/mar/25/united-learning-academy-chain-accuses-dfe-acting-illegally

12   Report in TES Jan 2018

13   Sue Cowley, first published in 2001 and into its fifth edition. Billed as 'The bestselling behavior management bible'

14   Education Executive January 2017. 'DfE says £3bn savings for schools 'doable' without larger class sizes'. https://edexec.co.uk/dfe-says-3bn-savings-for-schools-doable-without-larger-class-sizes/

15   Schools Week 28 April, 2019. *Forced out: The experienced teachers losing their livelihoods as schools cut costs.* https://schoolsweek.co.uk/forced-out-the-experienced-teachers-losing-their-livelihoods-as-schools-cut-costs/

16   Guardian 19 Apr 2019. Fifth of teachers plan to leave profession within two years. https://www.theguardian.com/education/2019/apr/16/fifth-of-teachers-plan-to-leave-profession-within-two-years

17   '10 reasons why Finland's education system is the best in the world', by Mike Colagrossi, originally published in *Big Think.* https://www.weforum.org/agenda/2018/09/10-reasons-why-finlands-education-system-is-the-best-in-the-world

18   The Education Reform Act of 1988 was the biggest shake

up for education since the 1944 Act. http://www.legislation.
gov.uk/ukpga/1988/40/pdfs/ukpga_19880040_en.pdf

19   See Maurice Plaskow's *Life and death of the Schools Council*,
Routledge Falmer, 1987.

20   Local Government Association (2018) Local services face
further 1.3 billion government funding cut in 2019/20.
https://www.local.gov.uk/about/news/local-services-face-
further-ps13-billion-government-funding-cut-201920

21   LGIU Local Government Information Unit, May 2018.
Policy Briefing on Academy Schools' finances – Public
Accounts committee https://www.lgiu.org.uk/wp-content/
uploads/2018/05/Academy-schools'-finances---Public-
Accounts-Committee.pdf

22   The report seems quite critical with conclusions like:
Academy trusts do not make enough information
available to help parents and local communities by the
start of the 2018/19 school year, [The DFE should] ensure
that all academy trusts have published complaints
procedures, including a named individual for parents
to escalate concerns to make clear and easily accessible
the name and contact details of whom in the Department
parents should turn to if their concerns are not addressed
adequately by the academy trust. ESFA is not sufficiently
transparent about the results of inquiries into concerns
about the financial management and governance of academy
trusts https://publications.parliament.uk/pa/cm201719/cms
elect/cmpubacc/1597/159705.htm#_idTextAnchor002

23   Wikipedia's account of the Organisation for Economic
and Cultural Development (OECD) and International
Association for the Evaluation of Educational Achievement
(IEA) promotion of measurement schemes is instructive:
Programme for International Student Assessment (PISA);
Trends in International Mathematics and Science Study
(TIMMS); and Progress in International Reading Literacy

Study (PIRLS). International comparisons are published annually for one or more of these curriculum areas. https://en.wikipedia.org/wiki/Programme_for_International_Student_Assessment

24   Innocenti Report Card 13 – Children in the Developed World (UNICEF, 2016) https://downloads.unicef.org.uk/wp-content/uploads/2016/04/RC13-ENG-FINAL.pdf?_ga=2.37076392.960960316.1556372959-1026048822.1556211489

25   https://www.theguardian.com/education/2016/dec/06/english-schools-core-subject-test-results-international-oecd-pisa

26   OECD (Nov 2017). *How does the United Kingdom compare on child well-being?* https://www.oecd.org/els/family/CWBDP_Factsheet_GBR.pdf

27   https://www.dailymail.co.uk/news/article-6627527/More-one-10-secondary-schools-performing.html

28   Sun newspaper Bad Education, 13 December, 2018. https://www.thesun.co.uk/news/7972670/full-list-england-worst-primary-schools-released/

29   https://fullfact.org/education/how-do-selective-school-ratings-compare/

30   A report from 2013 but little has changed. https://www.suttontrust.com/research-paper/poor-grammar-entry-grammar-schools-disadvantaged-pupils-england/

31   Guardian 7 Oct 2018. Tens of Thousands of children in England rejected for mental health treatment. https://www.theguardian.com/society/2018/oct/07/tens-of-thousands-of-children-in-england-rejected-for-mental-health-treatment

32   The Education Policy Institute report, School Performance in Academy Chains and Local Authorities – 2017. https://epi.org.uk/publications-and-research/performance-academy-local-authorities-2017/

33   DfE (2017) Experimental Statistics: Multi-academy trust

performance measures: England 2015 to 2016. https://assets. publishing.service.gov.uk/government/uploads/system/ uploads/attachment_data/file/584075/SFR02_2017.pdf

34 The House of Commons Committee of Public Accounts (January 2019) *Academy accounts and performance* https:// publications.parliament.uk/pa/cm201719/cmselect/ cmpubacc/1597/1597.pdf

35 LGA (2018) *Inspection Statistics: LA Maintained Schools and Academies.* https://www.local.gov.uk/sites/default/files/ documents/Academies%20and%20LA%20maintained%20 schools%20-%20June%202018%20Minor%20Revisions.pdf

36 Jess Staufenberg, *Schools Week* 23 May 2019, Failing schools more likely to improve under LA control. https:// schoolsweek.co.uk/failing-schools-more-likely-to-improve-under-la-control-new-study-claims/

37 House of Commons (2017) *Grammar School Statistics,* Briefing Paper 1398

38 'Flawed' Privatisation of Probation Services. https://www. huffingtonpost.co.uk/entry/probation-services-grayling_ uk_5cdc5221e4b0337da4ac411f

39 A. Wolf (2011) *Review of Vocational Education* https://assets. publishing.service.gov.uk/government/uploads/system/ uploads/attachment_data/file/180504/DFE-00031-2011.pdf

40 Institute of Public Policy Research (2018) *Prosperity and Justice: a plan for a new economy.* https://www.ippr.org/ files/2018-08/1535639099_prosperity-and-justice-ippr-2018. pdf

41 Schools Week, 01.03.19. Investigation: The highs (and occasional lows) of academy CEO pay https://schoolsweek. co.uk/investigation-the-highs-and-occasional-lows-of-academy-ceo-pay/

42 *Mailonline* 24 July, 2016 Academy bosses are spending thousands of taxpayers' money. https://www.dailymail. co.uk/news/article-3705746/Academy-bosses-spend-

thousands-taxpayers-money-luxury-services.html   More is available on this: *The Governor* Taxpayers fund large wages & lavish perks of academy school chiefs. http://www.thegovernor.org.uk/freedownloads/acadamies/Taxpayers%20fund%20large%20wages%20and%20lavish%20perks%20of%20academy%20school%20chiefs.pdf

43   853 Blog Parents' fury over academy chain's cutbacks at Brooklands School, 20 May, 2019. https://853london.com/2019/05/20/parents-fury-at-academy-chains-cutbacks-at-brooklands-primary-school/

44   Read Sonia Sodha's 'The great academy schools scandal', *Guardian*, 22 July 2018. https://www.theguardian.com/education/2018/jul/22/academy-schools-scandal-failing-trusts

45   J. Staufenberg. *Schools Week*, 11 Jan 2018. https://schoolsweek.co.uk/perry-beeches-academy-trust-closes-after-schools-move-to-new-sponsors/

46   Panorama 10 Sept 2018. *'Profits Before Pupils? The Academies Scandal'* on BBC iPlayer:https://www.bbc.co.uk/programmes/b0bk5q99

47   The sixth former's petition: https://www.change.org/p/hold-paul-murphy-to-account-for-his-actions

48   South London Press 20 Nov 2018. 'Student stands up to academy chain managing his school amid tax probe by government watchdog'. https://www.londonnewsonline.co.uk/student-stands-up-to-academy-chain-that-runs-his-school-amid-government-investigation-into-mat-finances/ The ESFA Report is at: https://assets.publishing.service.gov.uk/government/uploads/system/uploads/attachment_data/file/752998/Investigation_report_-_Education_for_the_21st_Century.pdf

49   Speech made by Michael Gove, then Secretary of State for Education, in Birmingham, January 2012. http://www.ukpol.

co.uk/michael-gove-2012-speech-to-schools-network/

50   A related party transaction is a transaction that takes place between two parties who hold a pre-existing connection prior to the transaction and may benefit unfairly and improperly.

51   TES 21 Nov, 2018. 'Exclusive: "Colossal £500,000 wasted per school, claims minister"'.https://www.tes.com/news/exclusive-colossal-ps500000-wasted-school-claims-minister

52   W. Mansell in *Education Uncovered* under the title, 'Academy, investigate thyself'. 14 June, 2017. https://www.educationuncovered.co.uk/themes/accountability-stories/124806/academy-investigate-thyself.thtml

53   Schools Week, 16 April, 2019. 'Exposed: the academy trust chief who boasted he "flicked away" safeguarding concerns'. https://schoolsweek.co.uk/exposed-the-academy-trust-chief-who-boasted-he-flicked-away-safeg uarding-concerns/

54   Anne West and David Wolfe, LSE Education Research Group, Academies, the School System in England and a Vision for theFuture. http://www.lse.ac.uk/social-policy/Assets/Documents/PDF/Research-reports/Academies-Vision-Report.pdf

55   Shenley Academy Ofsted Report 23-24 October 2018. School judged 'inadequate'. https://files.api.ofsted.gov.uk/v1/file/50045536

56   McGauran, A. & Mansell, W. (2017) *Free school sought to limit number of special needs and additional English speakers.* https://londonfoodbank.files.wordpress.com/2018/03/eu1.pdf. There is also a 2016 NUT paper *Free School provider with links to offshore company*, which reports that, in 2015, BPET (Belleview Place Education Trust) paid Bellevue Education £37,701 for the provision of school improvement services. https://www.whpara.org.uk/resources/The-School/WPS/NUT-Bellevue-Report.pdf. That is another story, as easily

brushed aside as all the rest.

57   Schools Week 9 Aug 2016. £2bn fund revealed for DfE free school property company. https://schoolsweek.co.uk/2bn-fund-revealed-for-dfe-free-school-property-company/

58   The dating agency was registered to the Durand Academy address, with Saffron tweeting and scantily clad women in The Coterie for private members to view. https://www.telegraph.co.uk/news/2016/06/03/sir-greg-martin-the-superhead-who-fell-from-grace-fights-back/

59   Schools Week 27 May, 2019. Ex-minister's academy trust ignores governance guidelines (which he wrote). https://schoolsweek.co.uk/ex-ministers-academy-trust-ignores-governance-guidelines/

60   Deborah Philips, 'Education free for all' in Rudd, T. and Goodson I., *Negotiating neoliberalism: developing alternative educational visions.* (Sense Publishers 2017)

61   Halley Academy redundancies News Shopper 23 January, 2019 https://www.newsshopper.co.uk/news/17378159.halley-academy-set-for-redundancies-to-avoid-falling-into-deficit/

62   Tammy Campbell, Ludovica Gambaro and Kitty Stewart (2019) *Inequalities in the experience of early education in England: Access, peer groups and transitions.* LSE/CASE Paper 2014. http://sticerd.lse.ac.uk/dps/case/cp/casepaper214.pdf

63   Guardian, 7 May, 2019. 'Cleansed by cuts'. https://www.theguardian.com/education/2019/may/07/cuts-heads-refuse-school-places-pupils-special-needs

64   *Teaching the Buggers to Behave* is the title of a book published by Sue Cowley in 2000. Several other '*Teaching the Buggers ...*' books have been published since.

65   Words reportedly uttered by Sir Dan Moynihan, Chief Executive of the Harris Academy Chain.

66   No talking in corridors is reported by the head of Albany to have led to a 10% spike in GCSEs and fewer pupils in

Isolation for poor behaviour. https://inews.co.uk/news/education/gcse-results-day-2018-school-banned-talking-corridors-increase/

67   BBC Panorama broadcast *Profits before Pupils? The Academies Scandal*, September, 2018 and *The Academy Schools Scandal*, March 2019.

About the authors

Terry Edwards (Teacher's Cert) is a retired secondary school teacher with 41 years of teaching experience in London schools.

Carl Parsons (BSc LSE, PhD Leeds) was a teacher and researcher and is a retired Professor of Education who has written about poverty and education, exclusions and the ills of inspection.

CULTURE, SOCIETY & POLITICS

The modern world is at an impasse. Disasters scroll across our smartphone screens and we're invited to like, follow or upvote, but critical thinking is harder and harder to find. Rather than connecting us in common struggle and debate, the internet has sped up and deepened a long-standing process of alienation and atomization. Zer0 Books wants to work against this trend. With critical theory as our jumping off point, we aim to publish books that make our readers uncomfortable. We want to move beyond received opinions.

Zer0 Books is on the left and wants to reinvent the left. We are sick of the injustice, the suffering, and the stupidity that defines both our political and cultural world, and we aim to find a new foundation for a new struggle.

If this book has helped you to clarify an idea, solve a problem or extend your knowledge, you may want to check out our online content as well. Look for Zer0 Books: Advancing Conversations in the iTunes directory and for our Zer0 Books YouTube channel.

Popular videos include:

Žižek and the Double Blackmain

The Intellectual Dark Web is a Bad Sign

Can there be an Anti-SJW Left?

Answering Jordan Peterson on Marxism

Follow us on Facebook
at https://www.facebook.com/ZeroBooks and Twitter at https://
twitter.com/Zer0Books

Bestsellers from Zer0 Books include:

Give Them An Argument
Logic for the Left
Ben Burgis
Many serious leftists have learned to distrust talk of logic. This is
a serious mistake.
Paperback: 978-1-78904-210-8 ebook: 978-1-78904-211-5

Poor but Sexy
Culture Clashes in Europe East and West
Agata Pyzik
How the East stayed East and the West stayed West.
Paperback: 978-1-78099-394-2 ebook: 978-1-78099-395-9

An Anthropology of Nothing in Particular
Martin Demant Frederiksen
A journey into the social lives of meaninglessness.
Paperback: 978-1-78535-699-5 ebook: 978-1-78535-700-8

In the Dust of This Planet
Horror of Philosophy vol. 1
Eugene Thacker
In the first of a series of three books on the Horror of Philosophy,
In the Dust of This Planet offers the genre of horror as a way of
thinking about the unthinkable.
Paperback: 978-1-84694-676-9 ebook: 978-1-78099-010-1

The End of Oulipo?
An Attempt to Exhaust a Movement
Lauren Elkin, Veronica Esposito
Paperback: 978-1-78099-655-4 ebook: 978-1-78099-656-1

Capitalist Realism
Is There No Alternative?
Mark Fisher
An analysis of the ways in which capitalism has presented itself
as the only realistic political-economic system.
Paperback: 978-1-84694-317-1 ebook: 978-1-78099-734-6

Rebel Rebel
Chris O'Leary
David Bowie: every single song. Everything you want to know,
everything you didn't know.
Paperback: 978-1-78099-244-0 ebook: 978-1-78099-713-1

Kill All Normies
Angela Nagle
Online culture wars from 4chan and Tumblr to Trump.
Paperback: 978-1- 78535-543-1 ebook: 978-1-78535-544-8

Cartographies of the Absolute
Alberto Toscano, Jeff Kinkle
An aesthetics of the economy for the twenty-first century.
Paperback: 978-1-78099-275-4 ebook: 978-1-78279-973-3

Malign Velocities
Accelerationism and Capitalism
Benjamin Noys
Long listed for the Bread and Roses Prize 2015, *Malign Velocities*
argues against the need for speed, tracking acceleration
as the symptom of the ongoing crises of capitalism.
Paperback: 978-1-78279-300-7 ebook: 978-1-78279-299-4

Meat Market
Female Flesh under Capitalism
Laurie Penny
A feminist dissection of women's bodies as the fleshy fulcrum of
capitalist cannibalism, whereby women are both consumers and
consumed.
Paperback: 978-1-84694-521-2 ebook: 978-1-84694-782-7

Babbling Corpse
Vaporwave and the Commodification of Ghosts
Grafton Tanner
Paperback: 978-1-78279-759-3 ebook: 978-1-78279-760-9

New Work New Culture
Work we want and a culture that strengthens us
Frithjoff Bergmann
A serious alternative for mankind and the planet.
Paperback: 978-1-78904-064-7 ebook: 978-1-78904-065-4

Romeo and Juliet in Palestine
Teaching Under Occupation
Tom Sperlinger
Life in the West Bank, the nature of pedagogy and the role of a university under occupation.
Paperback: 978-1-78279-637-4 ebook: 978-1-78279-636-7

Ghosts of My Life
Writings on Depression, Hauntology and Lost Futures
Mark Fisher
Paperback: 978-1-78099-226-6 ebook: 978-1-78279-624-4

Sweetening the Pill
or How We Got Hooked on Hormonal Birth Control
Holly Grigg-Spall
Has contraception liberated or oppressed women?
Sweetening the Pill breaks the silence on the dark side of hormonal contraception.
Paperback: 978-1-78099-607-3 ebook: 978-1-78099-608-0

Why Are We The Good Guys?
Reclaiming your Mind from the Delusions of Propaganda
David Cromwell
A provocative challenge to the standard ideology that Western power is a benevolent force in the world.
Paperback: 978-1-78099-365-2 ebook: 978-1-78099-366-9

The Writing on the Wall
On the Decomposition of Capitalism and its Critics
Anselm Jappe, Alastair Hemmens
A new approach to the meaning of social emancipation.
Paperback: 978-1-78535-581-3 ebook: 978-1-78535-582-0

Enjoying It
Candy Crush and Capitalism
Alfie Bown
A study of enjoyment and of the enjoyment of studying. Bown asks what enjoyment says about us and what we say about enjoyment, and why.
Paperback: 978-1-78535-155-6 ebook: 978-1-78535-156-3

Color, Facture, Art and Design
Iona Singh
This materialist definition of fine-art develops guidelines for architecture, design, cultural-studies and ultimately social change.
Paperback: 978-1-78099-629-5 ebook: 978-1-78099-630-1

Neglected or Misunderstood
The Radical Feminism of Shulamith Firestone
Victoria Margree
An interrogation of issues surrounding gender, biology, sexuality, work and technology, and the ways in which our imaginations continue to be in thrall to ideologies of maternity and the nuclear family.
Paperback: 978-1-78535-539-4 ebook: 978-1-78535-540-0

How to Dismantle the NHS in 10 Easy Steps (Second Edition)
Youssef El-Gingihy
The story of how your NHS was sold off and why you will have to buy private health insurance soon. A new expanded second edition with chapters on junior doctors' strikes and government blueprints for US-style healthcare.
Paperback: 978-1-78904-178-1 ebook: 978-1-78904-179-8

Digesting Recipes
The Art of Culinary Notation
Susannah Worth
A recipe is an instruction, the imperative tone of the expert, but
this constraint can offer its own kind of potential. A recipe need
not be a domestic trap but might instead offer escape – something
to fantasise about or aspire to.
Paperback: 978-1-78279-860-6 ebook: 978-1-78279-859-0

Most titles are published in paperback and as an ebook.
Paperbacks are available in traditional bookshops. Both print and
ebook formats are available online.
Follow us on Facebook
at https://www.facebook.com/ZeroBooks
and Twitter at https://twitter.com/Zer0Books